County Durham's Lost Houses

A picture postcard history by Jim Davidson

WAGTAIL PRESS

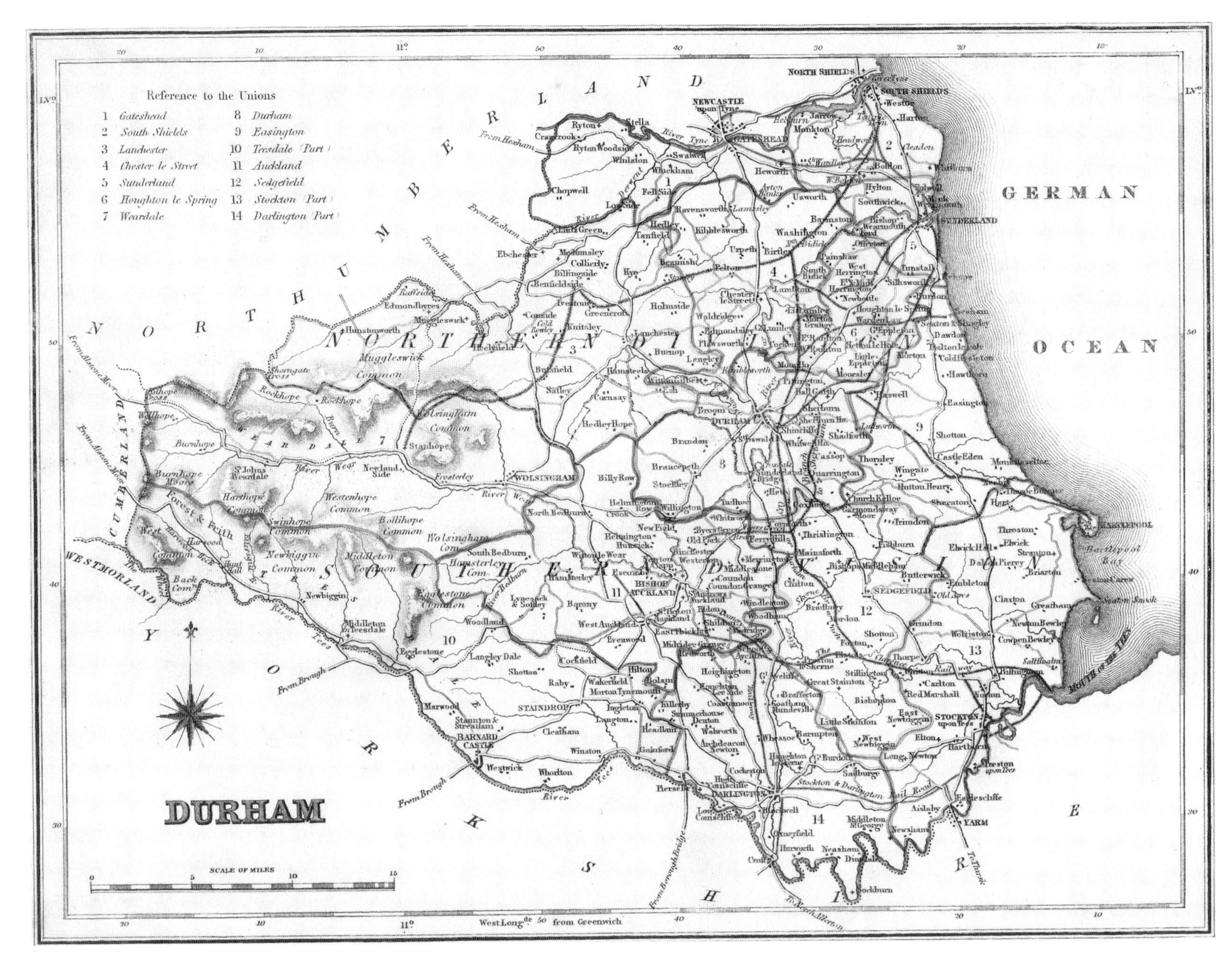

The historic boundary of County Durham, circa 1840.

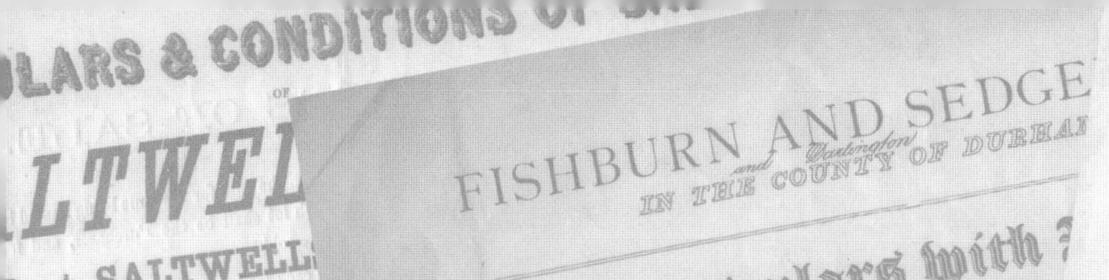

...LARS & CONDITIONS OF SA...
OF
...LTWEL...
...D at SALTWELL...
WHICH WILL B...
...SALE B...
...Y MR. J. ...
...THE TURK'S...
GREY STREET, NEWCA...
...TUESDAY, MA...
AT THREE O'CLOCK IN THE A...
...SOLD, THE PROPERTY WIL...
PARTICUL...
...hat valuable Freehold Estate of Saltwe...
...am, comprising the Mansion House know...
...ouses, Stabling, Coach Houses, Gardener...
...gs, with the Arable and Pasture Lands...
..., Esq., and others, the whole containing an...
...not Sold in One Lot it will be offered as fol...
...ot 1.—The Mansion House, Shrubberies, G...
...ener's Cottage, Lodge, Farm House, and ...
...Saltwell Lane to the Team Valley Railway...

FISHBURN AND SEDGE... and Darlington
IN THE COUNTY OF DURHAM
Particulars with ...
OF A
VALUABLE FREEHOL...
(Free of Land Tax, except a Nomin...
SITUATE IN THE
Township of Fishburn, and in the Parish of Sedg...
CALLED
"THE FISHBURN...
Consisting of a CAPITAL and COMMODIOUS M...
AND
SEVERAL FARM HOUSES AN...
TWO WELL-ACCUSTO...
THE BEEHIVE & ...
And 665 Acres, 0 Rood...
EXCELLENT ARABLE, M...
WITH THE VALUABLE SEAMS O...
AND ALSO OF A FA...
SITUATE IN THE TOW...
Consisting of a DWELLING HOUSE, and O...
of Excellent ...
And several closes of Freehold ...
WILL BE OFFE...
In pursuance of instructions recei...
BY M...

VALUABLE LEASEHOLD E...
IN THE COUNTY OF DURHAM
PARTICULARS AND CONDITIONS OF
OF A
LEASEHOLD ESTATE
CALLED
MOORHOUS...
SITUATE IN THE
PARISH OF HOUGHTON-LE-SPRING, IN THE COUNTY OF ...
LATE THE PROPERTY OF JOHN DUNN, ESQ., DECEASED,
(Distant about 3 Miles from the City of Durham, 9 from Sunderland, ...
Newcastle-upon-Tyne),
CONSISTING OF
AN EXCELLENT FAMILY RESIDENCE,
AND UPWARDS OF
95 ACRES OF ARABLE, MEADOW, PASTURE,
WOOD LANDS,
IN FIRST-RATE CULTIVATION,
WHICH WILL BE OFFERED
FOR SALE BY AUCTION,
BY MESSRS. SMALL AND BROUGH,
AT MRS. WARD'S, WATERLOO HOTEL, DURHAM,
On Friday, the 3d Day of February, 1843, ...

County Durham's Lost Houses

A picture postcard history by Jim Davidson

County Durham's Lost Houses

Contents

Foreword by Viscount Allendale

"It is a privilege to write a forword for Jim Davidson's follow-up book to his '**Northumberland's Lost Houses**'. For Jim to repeat this exercise for County Durham is a true public service, given the amount of research and hard work it must have taken.

We now have a record of what was in County Durham in the past and hopefully we won't lose any more of these remarkable examples of our heritage.

The Viscount Allendale
Bywell Castle
March 2022

Introduction

My home town of Dunston-on-Tyne was fairly typical of the many towns and villages throughout the old county of Durham that had developed before the local authority boundary changes introduced in 1974.

Throughout England during the fourteenth and fifteenth centuries the wealthier land owning families had established their estates under Kings and Bishops and little changed over the next few hundred years.

Prior to nineteen hundred the village of Dunston mainly kept to its early boundaries alongside the south bank of the River Tyne, with a greater concentration of buildings by the mouth of the River Team, known to all old Dunstonians as 'The Gut'. This pre nineteen hundreds Dunston was still encircled by the long established gardens, parks, and farmland attached to the estates of Redheugh, Farnacres, Ravensworth, Dunston Hill and Dunston Lodge. Of these, only the house at Dunston Hill survives today, the other lost houses all appearing in the following gazetteer.

The Dunston Hill Estate was bought by John Carr in 1704 from the Shafto family whose home it had been for over two hundred years. Carr was a mining operator and land agent and wished to establish himself as head of a new county family. He died in 1739 and his son Ralph Carr immediately began to re-front and enlarge the seventeenth century house which he had inherited. He also began to decorate and furnish his new Georgian rooms in a style befitting his newly acquired gentry status.

Richard Welford in his 'Men of Mark Twixt Tyne and Tweed', 1895, tells us: *"He purchased from his friend Sir John Dick, who had acquired it during a long residence as British Consul at Leghorn, a fine collection of old paintings and statuary, and added to his library valuable works which are still in the possession of his descendants."*

As well as enhancing the interior of Dunston Hill Ralph set about enlarging the estate and planting his gardens and parkland. Ralph Carr-Eliison's 'The Family of Carr', 1893-99 tells us: *"In 1750 he also enlarged the grounds by diverting the Whickham and Dunston turnpike road from the west to the east side of the freehold field called The Front Field."* Also, *"A further alteration of the Whickham Road was made in 1762, for the sake of making another addition to the park at Dunston Hill."*

The same book tells us: *"Memoranda exist at Dunston Hill of the fruit and timber trees planted by Ralph Carr in his earlier life, including the walnuts and Spanish chestnuts near the high nutwood, and the cherry trees to the north of the house."*

I can remember eating those walnuts and chestnuts as a young boy.

Fiona Green in 'A guide to the Historic Parks and Gardens of Tyne and Wear', 1995, tells us: *"The remains of a Ha-Ha are evident and magnificent trees are dispersed through the fields. The park also once boasted an ice-house and a large orchard."*

In 1870 Ralph Carr inherited through his mother the Ellison estates and became Ralph Carr-Ellison. Dunston Hill remained home to the Carr-Ellison family until the outbreak of the First World War. It had been further enlarged in 1782 but the family removed to their Northumberland house, Hedgely Hall, which they had greatly extended in 1874. Fireplaces and internal doors from Dunston Hill and the old Ellison seat of Hebburn Hall were incorporated into this extension work. The Ellisons had occupied Hebburn from 1650 until 1860.

The house and grounds of Dunston Hill were turned by the family into an after care home for disabled soldiers and sailors. This private family venture was soon turned over to the Northumberland War Pensions Committee and turned fully into a hospital for the war wounded. I can still remember the blue serge suited old soldiers smoking at the now demolished lodge on Whickham Highway up to the 1960s. At the end of the war the house became a Nurses Home for the staff who serviced the hospital housed in wooden wards in the grounds. The walled garden was restored in 1995. Hospital use was followed

DUNSTON HILL

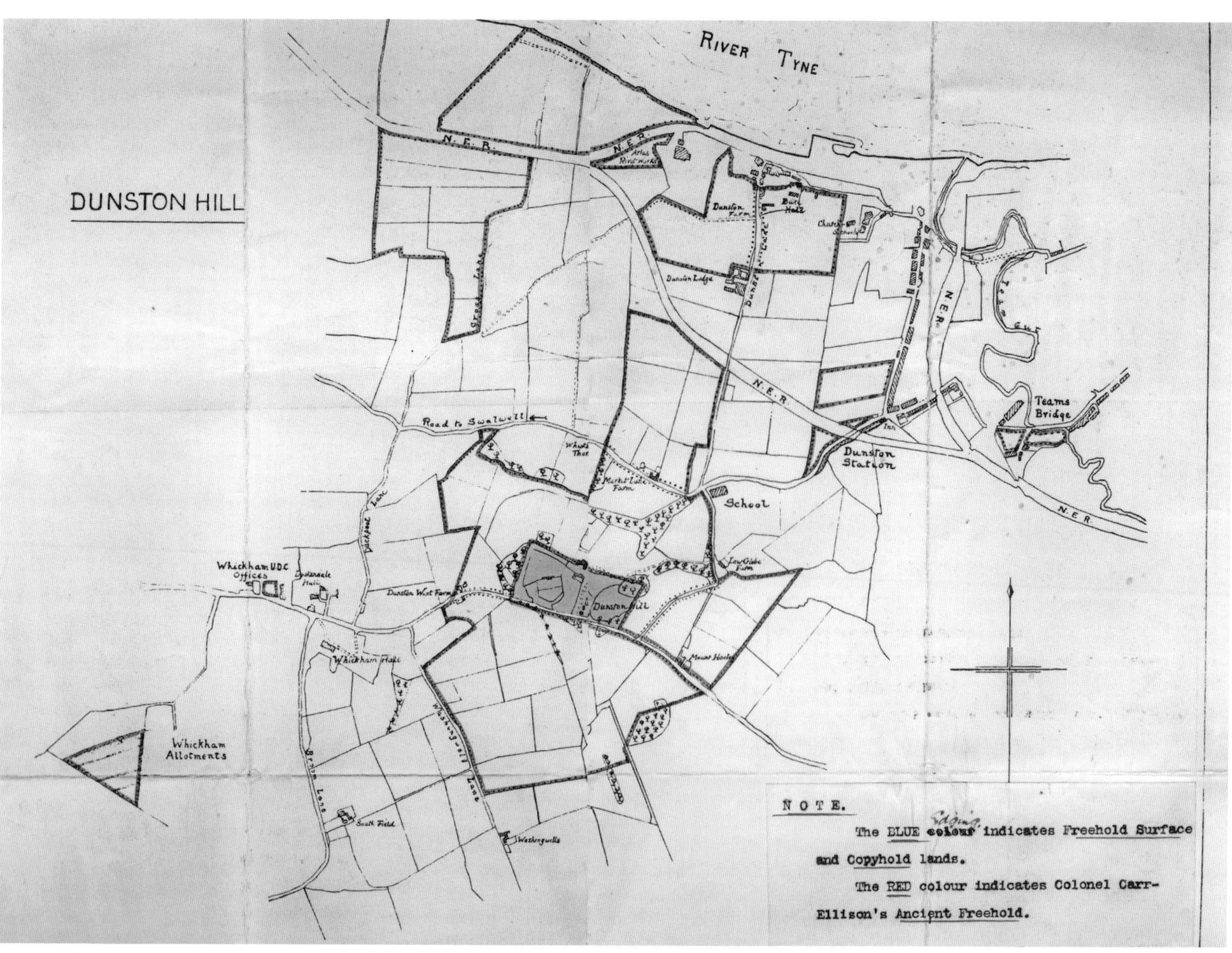

Dunston Hill Estate.

by a long period of emptiness and neglect but the house has now been converted into luxury apartments with housing development in the grounds.

The 1858 Ordnance Survey map of the Dunston area shows no fewer than nine working farms and Whellan's Directory of 1894 still shows four surviving. Today only three farmhouses survive, Dunston or Whitegate Farm, Dunston West or Dunston Hill Farm and Whickham Thorns. Non fulfil their original role as working farms although they make very fine houses. This pattern of change was typical of developments across County Durham. Park and farm land was gradually covered by housing, particularly on the edge of expanding towns like Gateshead and Darlington. Often the old landed families like the Carr-Ellisons of Dunston Hill and the Liddells of Ravensworth Castle would simply move to secondary seats further away from growing populations, industry and its accompanying urbanisation. The Carr-Ellisons moved to Hedgely Hall and the Liddells to Eslington Park, both in Northumberland and remain there today.

Frank Manders in his 'A History of Gateshead', 1973, confirms this view. Talking of Gateshead's old estates he says: *"Their houses, many of them of architectural interest, survived until the 1930s, when during a single decade, almost every private house of significance was demolished."*

This pattern of destruction was repeated throughout Durham and indeed England for the many small estates surrounding rapidly expanding towns, as G. A. Cowen confirms in 'The Braes of Derwent Hunt', 1955: *'"The one word coal can very largely account for the disappearance of the North Durham Hunt. The great developments of the collieries in the eastern half of the country, with the consequent spread of the population, made it largely unhuntable. Nearly all the big country houses became empty, or were diverted to other uses."* Robert Smith Surtees of Hamsterley Hall in Durham agreed. Surtees, the famous creator of 'Jorrocks', thought that Durham was *"A glorious country to hunt"*, but that *"it must soon be ruined through colliery and railway expansion."* Una Pope-Hennessy in her 'Durham Company' held the same view. Talking of Robert Surtees of Mainsforth, famous Durham antiquarian and friend of Sir Walter Scott and Robert Southey, she called Mainsforth Hall *"An island site in an implacable waste of coalfields."* Poor old Mainsforth Hall was demolished in 1962 after standing empty for several years.

Dunston's own industries were also rapidly expanding. Sadler's boat building establishment founded in the late seventeen hundreds was followed by Palmer's Timber Yard in the eighteen hundreds. Crowley Millington's nail making business soon followed along with many smaller businesses. Expansion was hampered by larger river craft only being able to navigate the River Tyne as far inland as Gateshead. 'Kings Meadows' island effectively blocked larger craft going further up stream. To the east of 'Kings Meadows' lay the smaller 'Clarence Islands' and to its west the even smaller 'Little Annie'. The Tyne improvement Commissioners were established in 1850 and in 1854 the foundation stones of the north and south piers were laid. Work then progressed up the Tyne, dredging, widening and straightening the course of the river.

By 1887 all of Dunston's islands had been dredged away, opening up the area to the future development of industry and transport systems. Dunston's most important industry was linked to coal. From its early small scale extraction in the fourteen hundreds to its deep mines opened in the eighteen seventies, Dunston stood at the forefront of the coal industry. More important than the actual mining of coal, Dunston was to become the major shipping point for the exportation of coal from the North Durham coalfield. Colliers left for London and the world from Dunston's most important industrial monument, Dunston Coal Staiths, possibly the largest wooden structure in the world, finally closing in 1980 but still surviving.

By 1914 when Dunston's population was circa nine thousand, W. J. Weston could write in his 'The County of Durham', 1914, that: *"Dunston, just below the junction*

Dunston Hill House.

of Derwent and Tyne, has within a few years become an important coal port, and owing to many new industries - there is a monster flour mill and a host of small foundries - it has a rapidly increasing population."

Also: *"At Dunston-on-Tyne practically the whole town belongs to the wage earners, where the houses are rapidly climbing up the hill overlooking the Tyne, and the double city, Newcastle and Gateshead."*

One hundred years later this prescient joining of Newcastle and Gateshead has almost become reality.

With the industrial development of Dunston and Gateshead came the need for many more houses for the workers. Cheaper to build terraced housing came first. This ranged from the one up, one down, netties or lavatories in the middle of the square, at 'Saddler Square', to the grand stone built 'The Crescent'. Increased pay for workers saw the growth of semi-detached houses and Local Authority housing was also built to high standards.

With all this house building came churches, chapels, schools and shops and Dunston's open spaces began to disappear. Dunston showed in microcosm what was happening throughout Durham and indeed many other parts of England expanding in the same way.

From agricultural beginnings, the development of industry, the growth of population and the subsequent loss of park and farmland that supported those old estates like Redheugh, Ravensworth and Dunston Lodge the landscape changed. The survival of the houses once at the centre of these estates throughout the county had mixed fortunes but in Dunston's case, due to its location on the outskirts of rapidly expanding Gateshead and Newcastle, only Dunston Hill survived.

The lost houses of the Dunston area ranged in size and importance from a seat of the nobility at Ravensworth Castle, an ancient gentry house at Redheugh Hall to the houses of local landowners represented by the Harrison family at Bute Hall, the Marley family at Dunston Lodge and the Archer family at Farnacres. Ravensworth Cottage also belonged in this category as does the surviving Whickham Hill now divided into two large houses.

Local industrialists' houses, slightly lower down the social ladder, also suffered losses. Ironically the industry which saw them built was also responsible in many cases for their demise. The Dixon family home of Team Villa disappeared, and Dunston House, home to the Atkinson family was demolished as recently as 2016. This house, in 1913, became Dunston House Mechanics Social Club and Institute and within five years had a membership of over six hundred. It was also known locally as 'The Abode of Love' - but that's a subject for another book.

Atlas Villa of 1889, home to the Whitfields, is now surrounded by light industry. Dunston Vicarage also survives but now sits alongside a house of circa 2000 built in its old walled garden. Many of County Durham's rectories and vicarages proved too large and expensive to maintain by modern clergy families and have either disappeared or been cheaply sold off by the Diocese to become highly desirable homes.

This pattern of loss was repeated throughout Durham County but more particularly in its northern half. South Durham away from industrial Teesside is still mainly rural and retains its great estates of Raby, Brancepeth, Wynyard and Windlestone. Its series of seventeenth century Tees Valley houses have also survived unscathed including Gainford, Snow Hall, Westholme, Sledwich, Greystone, Alwent, Selaby, Thornton, Headlam and Ulnaby.

The humble postcard, hugely popular in the early nineteen hundreds can often provide the only surviving visual record of a lost country house. What follows is a selection of postcard views of many of County Durham's lost large houses.

The following pages are a record of those many County Durham houses that didn't survive.

Gazetteer of Lost Houses

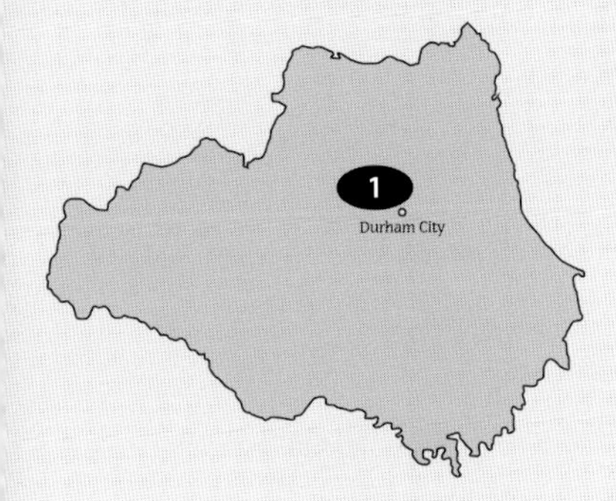

Acorn Close

SACRISTON. *c.1865 - c.1935*

1

Considering its position at the centre of Charlaw, Kimblesworth, Nettlesworth and Sacriston Collieries, it comes as no surprise to discover that in 1903 Acorn Close was home to Colonel William Blackett. The Colonel was manager of Sacriston Colliery and Acorn Close, described as 'A fine house with extensive grounds'. These grounds included orchards, greenhouses and fish ponds. Also tennis courts which provided tennis parties for friends and neighbours on a regular circuit of house visits. The position of Acorn Close led to its downfall. Subsidence from drift mine workings saw the house demolished circa 1935.

Ashbrooke House (later Corby Hall)

SUNDERLAND. *1864 - 1976*

2

Built by Sunderland born architect Thomas Moore in 1864 for James Hartley, glassmaker, who in 1836 built the largest and most modern glass works in the world at Millfield. Lived in by the Hartley family until 1886 and the shipbuilding Short family until 1932. In 1933 the house was bought by the Jesuits as a mens' retreat house, they renamed it Corby Hall after the Jesuit martyr Ralph Corby. The house was demolished in 1976 and replaced by flats. The house gave its name to Sunderland's most desirable suburb of Ashbrooke.

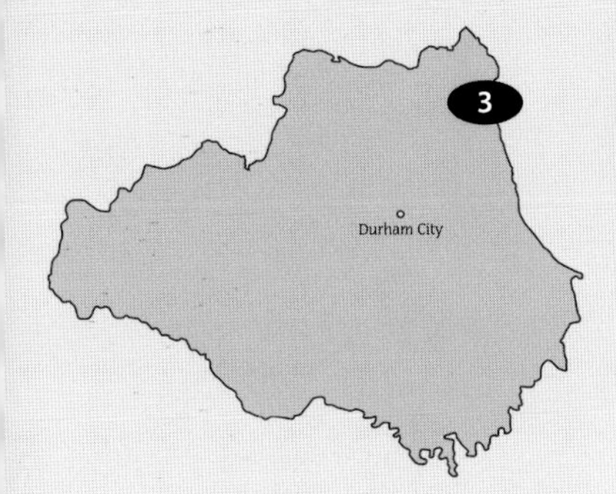

Belford Villas (later Belford House and Ashcroft)

SUNDERLAND. *c.1870s - 2006*

3

Belford Villa was home to Sir Robert Norman Thompson, shipbuilder, and his family from 1906 until his death in the 1950s. Ashcroft was home to a number of industrialists and ship owners including the engineer John Eric Steel. His expanding company acquired Coles Cranes and was to become one of Sunderland's largest employers.

Both of the huge gothic houses were set in large grounds with a bowling green and tennis courts as well as manicured gardens and grounds. They were both extended in 1910 and 1928. Belford House became a sports and social club before both villas were lost to fire in 2006.

Benfieldside House

SHOTLEY BRIDGE. - *c.1960*

4

Born in 1839 Richard Murray became a wealthy Shotley Bridge philanthropist and the owner of the North Eastern Breweries. He donated the site and sixty-thousand pounds to build the Richard Murray Hospital, laying the foundation stone in 1912, but he died before the opening in 1914.

His residence, Benfieldside House, was demolished circa 1960 and redeveloped as Benfield Close housing estate. Shotley Bridge is still surrounded by many fine houses such as Shotley Park, Derwent Lodge, Shotley Grove and, across the River Derwent in Northumberland, the high Victorian neo-gothic Shotley Hall, built in 1863 with its Edward Burne-Jones elements made by William Morris's firm.

Biddick Hall Lodge

WASHINGTON.

5

Biddick Hall still stands on the Lambton estate with its five bay main front, the centre bay flanked by giant pilasters. The pediment is topped by three vases and four more top the parapet. Parts of the house date from the sixteenth century but the major build is early eighteenth century. The baroque styling of the main facade has led to the suggestion that Sir John Vanbrugh had a hand in the design. He was working on neighbouring Lumley Castle in 1721.

From 1837 until 1932 the former Dower House of Lambton Castle had been used as the residence of the agent of the estate. In 1932 the Lambton family moved from the castle to Biddick and made it their home. Major demolition work on the castle in 1932 probably also saw the demise of the grand lodge shown above.

Durham City

6

Billingham Hall

BILLINGHAM. *c.1875 - 1935*

6

Demolished in 1935, Billingham Hall was home to a succession of local shipbuilders and ship owners. The site at Billingham Junction is now covered by housing but the house is survived by a lodge and gates.

Billingham Hall was a high Victorian house with two spire topped towers rising a floor above the rest of the house. These provided wonderful vantage points to view the gardens and surrounding countryside which was very quickly covered by the urban spread of Billingham.

Bird Hill House

WHICKHAM. - *1962*

7

Bourn's Annals of the Parish of Whickham tells us that on January 21st, 1825, "married at Gibside Chapel, by special license, John Davidson, of West Otterburn, Northumberland, and Susan Hussey Elizabeth Jessup of Bird Hill House near Whickham, grand daughter of John Lyon, 9th Earl of Strathmore". The happy couple moved to Ridley Hall in Northumberland. When last inhabited in 1958 Bird Hill House still had no water supply or electricity. The house had thirteen rooms plus servants quarters, offices and work rooms.

Birtley Hall

BIRTLEY. *1815 - altered 1843 - 1918*

8

Designed in 1815 by John Dobson and altered by him in 1843 for J. Warwick and lived in by successive managers of Birtley Iron Works. The Hall is survived by a lodge situated on Durham Road. The family photograph shows Miss Laverty from Hexham who was ' in service' at Birtley Hall circa 1913. She moved on to Southill in Chester-le-Street, Jesmond Grove in Newcastle, and finally to Sutton Hall in Thirsk, Yorkshire. Servants moved house regularly moving from the lowliest positions, hall boy, scullery maid etc., as a means of gaining promotion and higher wages.

Bishopwearmouth Grange

SUNDERLAND. *1784 -*

9

The Grange, built in 1784 for the Maling family, was the grandest classical house ever seen in Sunderland. Unfortunately it was built too near the town's centre to work as a country retreat and in 1830 it was converted into the Grange School. This was a private school run by Dr. James Cowan, an educationalist with a great reputation.

The house was next bought by George Hudson, a local philanthropist who in 1879 founded the George Hudson Charity for the education, maintenance and support of fatherless children aged eight to fourteen. He died at the Grange in 1884.

By 1851 Sunderland was twice the size of Durham, Gateshead, Hartlepool or South Shields, the next most important centres in County Durham. Building land was at a premium and the Grange was demolished and replaced by the Grange Estate, including the grand St. Georges Square, built in 1855 to the overall design of Martin Greener, a pupil and employee of John Dobson. This too is now sadly demolished, the beautiful gardens and grounds long gone.

Bishopwearmouth Rectory

SUNDERLAND. - *1855*

The Rector of Bishopwearmouth lived in some style, through revenues from a glebe of 130 acres and further parcels of land known as the Rectory Manor. The Rev. J.P. Eden, rector from 1848 to 1864 had the medieval rectory demolished and a new one built to the design of John Dobson. The grand staircase from the demolished building was incorporated into the Dobson replacement. Medieval features survived in the demolished rectory which had been rebuilt during the eighteenth century.

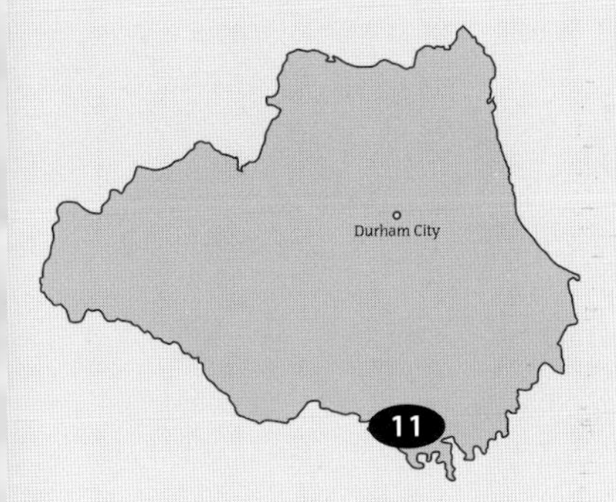

Blackwell Hall

DARLINGTON. *c.1780 - 1965*

11

Built for the Allan family but, together with the rest of their estate, was passed in 1885 to Sir Henry Havelock V.C., hero of the Battle of Lucknow. He subsequently became Sir Henry Havelock-Allan.

After a short time as a hotel the house was to be converted into apartments but was found to be structurally unsound. Demolition followed in 1965. The site is now occupied by the houses of Blackwell Grove.

Blackwell Hill

DARLINGTON. *1873 - c.1972*

12

Blackwell Hill was a red brick gothic villa with stone dressing designed by John Ross of Darlington for Eliza Barclay. Eliza was the sister of John Church Backhouse, head of the quaker banking dynasty. John Ross FRIBA (1836-95) also designed Brinkburn, Cockerton and Mowden Hall, as well as major alterations and additions to existing houses, conservatories being his speciality.

The site is now covered by the houses of Farrholme although the gate lodge still survives.

Blaydon Castle (later Turret Place)

BLAYDON. *C17th - 1926*

13

Blaydon Castle was built on Selby's Haugh, a haugh being an area of low lying land bordering a river and often prone to flooding. The lower Tyne valley had many haughs and probably the best known was at Stella, home to the famous Blaydon Races. The Selbys fell on hard times and in the late seventeenth century sold the estate, the bulk of the land passing to the Clavering family of neighbouring Axwell Park. The mansion of Axwell designed by James Paine in 1758 has been restored in recent years from its condition as a derelict shell. In the nineteenth century the castle was divided into tenements often occupied by Irish workers seeking work in England. The castle gradually deteriorated and was demolished in 1926. The site is now covered by an industrial estate.

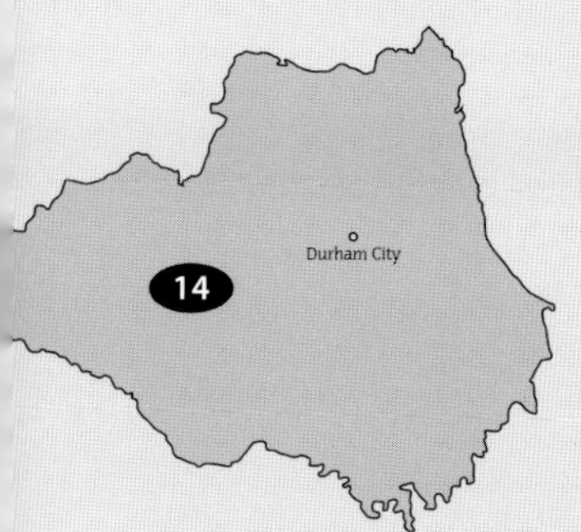

Bradley Hall

WOLSINGHAM.

14

Upper Weardale formed the Park of the Bishops of Durham with the medieval buildings at Eastgate and Westgate guarding the desmesne. The Bishops discouraged other building in the dale which might spoil their hunting pursuits but did allow the building of a medieval fortified house at Bradley, east of Wolsingham. This house was made more comfortable in Tudor times and was further altered into a Georgian country house.

The view of the sixteenth century house shows the change from fortified house to a symmetrical Tudor manor house with typical renaissance details with no thought of fortification. The view also shows that the house is in decay and a period of reduction followed. What is left today is a small Georgian house formed from the east side of the Tudor manor house. The house was home to several local families including the Eures, Tempests and Bowes.

Branksome Hall (formerly Westfield)

COCKERTON. - *1978*

15

The original Westfield shown to the right of the above view was greatly extended in the 1880s by the addition of an Elizabethan style west wing. A new entrance lodge and stable block were built at the same time. The house was home to the Kitching family from 1882 until 1948 when they moved to Hurworth Old Hall. Although listed, the house was demolished in 1978 following use as a warehouse and the park developed for housing.

16
Durham City

Broadwood Hall

SATLEY. *1875 - 1958*

16

Built in 1875 by Edward Taylor-Smith of Colepike Hall who was still hunting with the Braes of Derwent until into his eighties. He died at Broadwood in 1888 in his eighty-seventh year. The house was razed to the ground in 1961 by Tom Cowie, the Sunderland entrepreneur, knighted in 1992. The house was bought for £6,000, riddled with dry rot and still lit by oil lamps. It was replaced by a sixteen roomed mansion fitted with all mod cons.

Durham City

17

Brussleton Tower

ST. HELEN AUCKLAND. *c.1730 -1961*

17

The tower was probably built for William Carr of Cocken Hall who married Elizabeth Carr of St. Helen's Hall in 1731. The tower served as an eye catcher for St. Helen's Hall and took the form of an octagonal stone tower. A steep flight of external steps climbed to the tower's single room which contained very fine stucco work. Perhaps it was done at the same time that the Palladian wing, with its glorious stucco work, was added to St. Helen's Hall. The tower was gutted by fire in 1935 and demolished in 1961. A visit to the demolished Stella Hall in Blaydon, with its surviving fine octagonal summer house on Summer Hill, reminds us of what has been lost at Brussleton.

Building Hill House

SUNDERLAND. *c.1700 - c.1855*

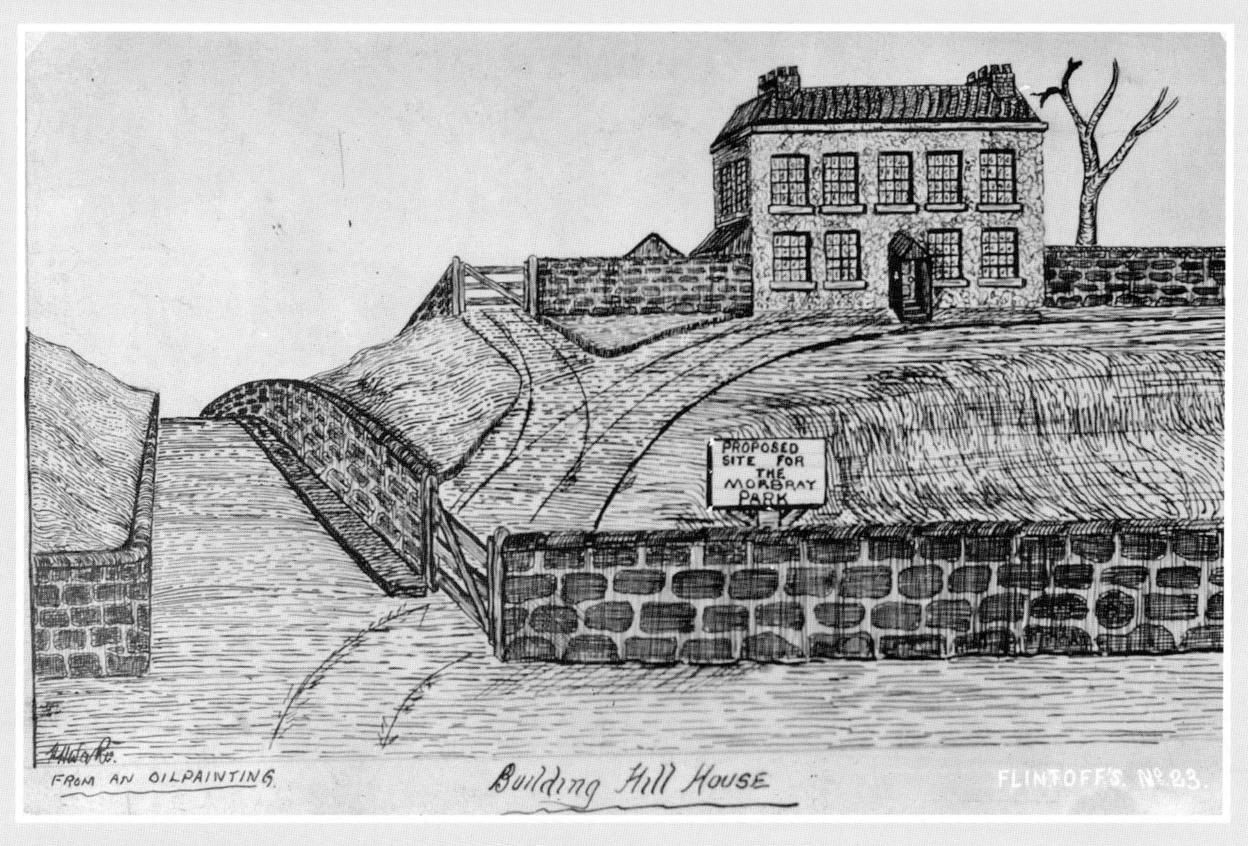

18

Building Hill House was demolished for the building of Mowbray Park. It occupied the site now used for the monument to Sir Henry Havelock, the hero of the Indian Mutiny campaign. Building Hill, where the town's building stone had been quarried before the availabilty of cheap bricks, was bought by Sunderland Corporation in 1854 from the Mowbray family for two thousand pounds and the park laid out. Mowbray Park opened in 1857 with a lodge and bandstand designed by William Crozier. The park was quickly extended and the reopening in 1866 involved a procession of seventeen thousand Sunday School children, watched by an estimated twenty thousand inhabitants.

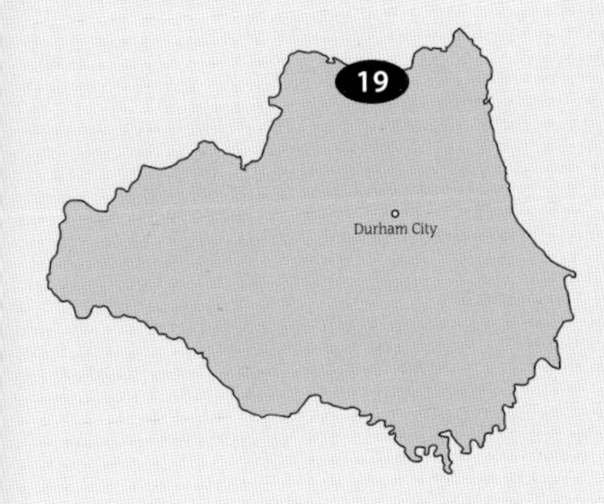

Bute Hall

DUNSTON. *c.1700 - 1958*

19

William Bourn's annals of the parish of Whickham tells us that: *"Bute Hall was built by Jasper Harrison esq., but seems to have undergone several alterations. Most of the rooms are large and some contain large fire places."*

In the 1940s the house was divided into tenements. The Bute connection arose when Lady Jane Clavering of Axwell Park's daughter, Alice, married the fourth Earl and later Marquis of Bute. This made the Marquis an hereditary grand ally in the vastly profitable coal trade of Tyneside.

As a boy I used to love exploring the empty house with my father.

Durham City

20

Castlegate Corner

STOCKTON. *c.1660 - 1907*

20

Demolished in 1907 when the Castle Theatre was built on the site. The houses were typical seventeenth century town houses with Elizabethan style windows, high chimneys and pantile roofs. These red pantiles were a feature of north-east England and south-east Scotland and came from Holland. They acted as ballast for the returning empty colliers. The pantiles are roof tiles with a curved 'S' shaped section and can still be seen on north-east houses from the lowliest cottage to the grandest mansion.

Cleadon Cottage (later Cleadon Park)

CLEADON. *Enlarged 1845 - 1981*

21

The original farm house on the site was converted for Robert Swinburne, glass maker, to the design of John Dobson in 1845. For the rest of the nineteenth and into the early twentieth century it served as home to a series of manufacturers. Charles Anderson, colliery owner; Peter Haggie, rope maker and finally James Kirkley who was a great benefactor of Cleadon Church.

The house ended its life as a sanatorium from 1922 until 1978. Demolition follwed in 1981 and the site covered by the housing of Parkshiel estate.

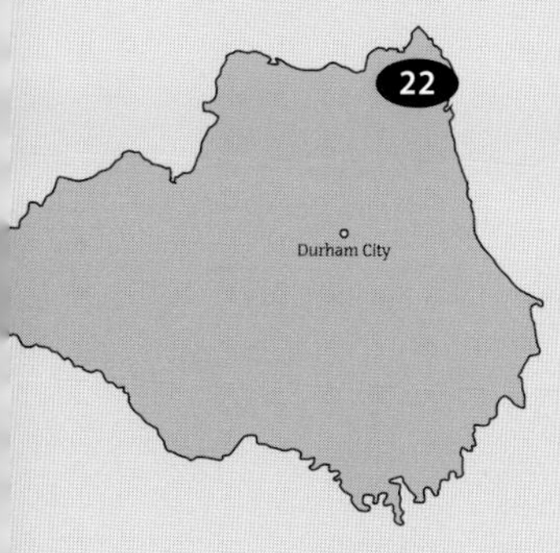

Cleadon Meadows

CLEADON. *1853 - c.1955*

22

Like many of its contemporaries Cleadon Meadows and its grounds have been covered by housing. In this case the Cleadon Meadows estate. The house was situated behind the Brittania Inn and was, in the late 1800s, home to Robert Lamb esq. In the 1880s it was owned by banker John Broderick Dale and his company was merged into Barclays Bank.

Cleadon Meadows was designed by John Dobson in 1853. Dobson was the most prolific country house builder in Durham and Northumberland during the nineteenth century.

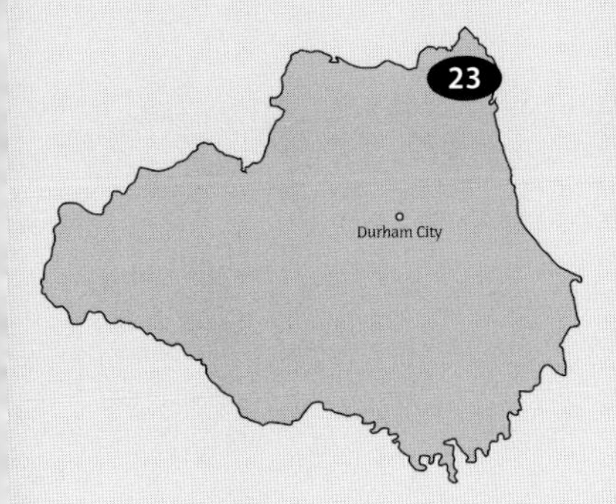

Cleadon Old Hall

CLEADON. *c.1720 - Refronted 1872 - 1936*

23

The Old Hall was situated in the centre of Cleadon, close to Cleadon Meadows. The house was refronted in 1872 with new bay windows and a roof balustrade to unify the frontage. In later years the house was known locally as Humble's Hall after James Humble, owner from 1908 to 1920.

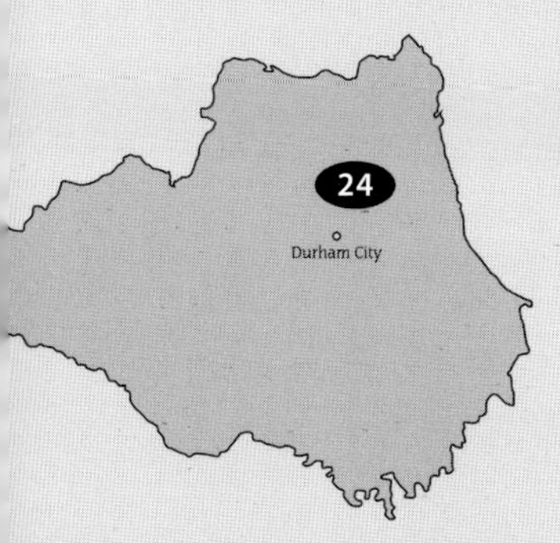

Cocken Hall

GREAT LUMLEY. *c.1680 -*

24

The Carrs and their descendants owned the Cocken estate from the seventeenth century until the early nineteenth century. Cocken Hall was illustrated by Johannes Kip and Leonard Knyff, circa 1710, for Ralph Carr. Cocken was the only Durham house and park to be illustrated by this prolific illustrating duo.

Cocken was hired by Carmelite nuns from 1804 until 1830, after living from 1794 until 1804 at St. Helen's Hall. The rent at Cocken proved too high and the nuns moved on to Cockerton Field House near Darlington.

In 1844 the house was halved in size, as shown in the illustration, and finally demolished in the 1900s.

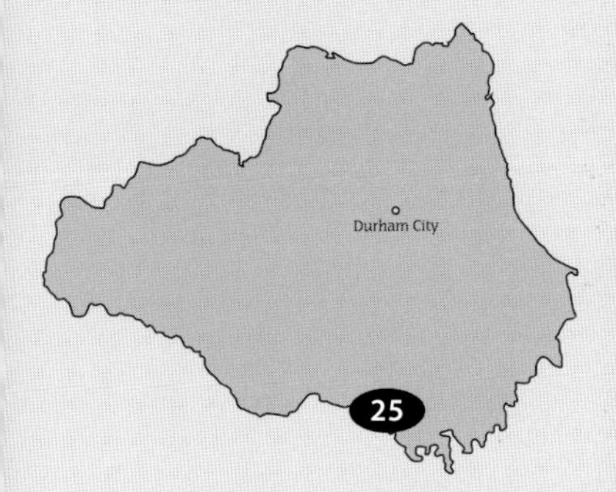

Conscliffe Hall

HIGH CONISCLIFFE.

25

It is very unusual to be able to trace the architectural history of a country house. Some alterations, such as a refronting, can alter a house beyond recognition. In the case of Conscliffe Hall the alterations are all too obvious. The three stages of alterations are formed only by additions and the three postcards show this clearly. The house was owned by the Westolls and was accidentally burned to the ground.

The vicarage which sits on top of the cliff, after which the village takes its name, was linked to the base of the cliff by a tower but unfortunately it has been drastically reduced in size.

Consett Hall

CONSETT. *c.1810 -*

26

One of the few Consett buildings to predate the establishment of Consett Iron Works in the early 1840s and was subsequently used for many years by the senior officials of that business. The house is mentioned in 1820 but the white brick, stone detailed gothic house shown above is obviously a much later replacement.

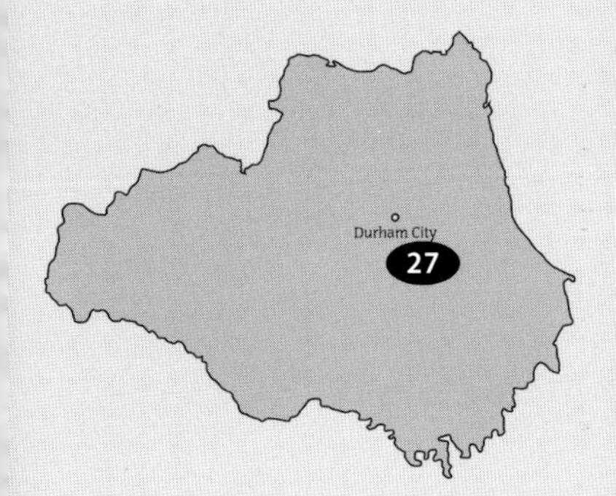

Coxhoe Hall

COXHOE. *c.1400 - Rebuilt 1725 - 1952*

27

Best known as the birthplace of Elizabeth Barrett Browning in 1806, the house was ornamented by James Paine for the Burdon family in 1754. He added the gothic windows and battlements. The fine plasterwork was also possibly by Paine and worked by Giuseppe Cortese who also worked at nearby Hardwick and Elemore Hall. Coxhoe was home to the Wood family from 1850 until 1938.

A press item which appeared on May 21st 1927 reads as follows: *"On the invitation of their president, Mr. John Wood J.P., Coxhoe Hall, the members of Coxhoe Motor Club visited Coxhoe Hall on Saturday afternoon where they were received by the president and, after being photographed, enjoyed a ramble through the delightful grounds and gardens. Subsequently a club run was held to High Force, England's highest waterfall."*

Crook Hall

CONSETT. *c.1690 -1900*

28

Named in Boldon Book, the seventeenth century house was home to the Shafto and Barker families. It ended its days owned by the Consett Iron Company and was dismantled circa 1900. Much of the stonework was used to build West Park in nearby Lanchester.

From 1794 until 1808 the Hall was used as a Roman Catholic seminary whilst Ushaw College was being built. Before this the refugee priests had been housed at Pontop Hall in Dipton.

Crowtree House

SUNDERLAND. *c.1700* -

29

One of several Georgian mansions which once surrounded Bishopwearmouth Green and which is shown on Rain's famous 'eye plan' of Sunderland done in 1785. The settlement of Bishopwearmouth was home to Sunderland's wealthiest inhabitants. But, as the nineteenth century progressed, it was gradually abandoned by its prosperous families, many of them moving to the developing suburb of Ashbrooke.

Crowtree House was owned by the Mowbray family who sold the house to Mr. Charles McKenzie for one thousand pounds in 1884. Shrewd Mr. McKenzie promptly sold the house to Sunderland School Board for one thousand, seven hundred and fifty pounds, nearly doubling his money. The School Board demolished the house and replaced it with a school.

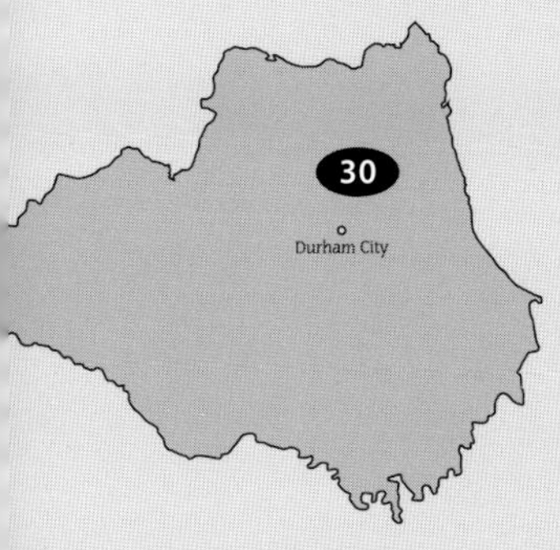

The Deanery

CHESTER-LE-STREET. *C16th - 1907*

30

Altered and extended by the Cookson family in the 1830s then later bought by Durham County Education Committee in 1906. In 1911 the school built on the site was opened. The entrance gates are also gone, does anyone know of their whereabouts?

Deneholme

HORDEN. - *1969*

31

Probably Victorian, Deneholme was a curious half octagonal shaped house with castellated wings. From 1895 Deneholme operated as a café with rooms to let for holidaymakers.

In 1910 the house was bought by Horden Collieries Ltd to accommodate trainee colliery officials.

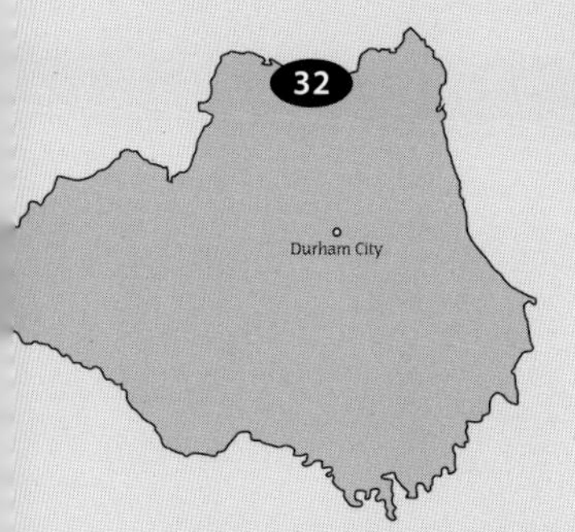

Dunston Lodge

DUNSTON. *c.1600 - 1911*

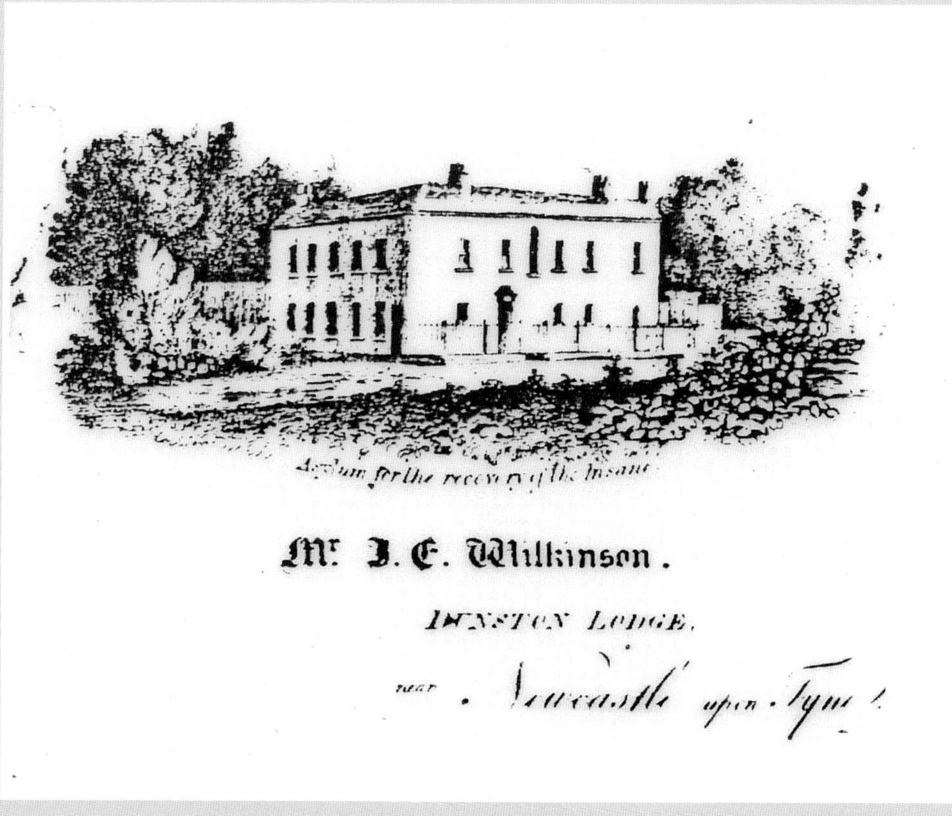

32

William Bourn tells us in his 'Whickham Parish' of 1893: *"Dunston Lodge was formerly held by the Marley family. It is an old mansion containing a great number of rooms."* Also: *"In 1773 died Robert Marley of Dunston Lodge, aged ninety-one years."*

In 1830 the house became a private lunatic asylum and enjoyed great success with over sixty percent of its patients discharged recovered. Cornelius Garbutt became proprietor in 1852 and his son William took over in 1865 until its closure in 1900. The estate was then run as a market garden by the Kennedy family when only a small part of the house remained suitable for habitation. Today the site is covered by the Meadow Lane housing estate, West Park, and the present Dunston Lodge, a pleasant 1930s villa.

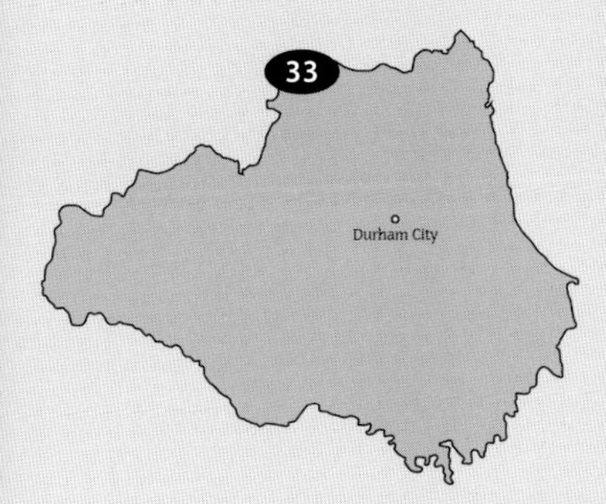

Elvaston Hall

RYTON. *c.1880 -*

33

Elvaston was home to Charles Algernon Parsons from 1884 until 1894. He was the son of the third Earl of Rosse and served a senior apprenticeship at W. G. Armstrong's Elswick works followed by a time at Clarke Chapman's in Gateshead. Parsons began experimenting on steam turbine engines and in 1889 he established his own company in Heaton. His experiments resulted with the steam launch 'Turbinia' which amazed the crowds at the Spithead naval review by travelling at the unprecedented speed of thirty-four and a half knots. Within ten years of Turbinia's great success the 'Mauretania' was built powered by seventy thousand horse power steam turbine engines. Parsons partly credited this success to his earlier experiments with model boats on Ryton duck pond. The card shows his children, Rachael Mary and Algernon George, in the family trap in front of Elvaston. He spent his last years at Ray Demesne, a Northumberland mansion which is now demolished.

34

Eshwood Hall

NEW BRANCEPETH. *1874 - 1927*

34

A sixty acre estate with twenty acres of gardens with ponds, waterfalls, rockeries and garden stone work, all laid out by owner Henry Heath Cochrane. He imported soil, peat and sand to transform the gardens which, according to sale plans, included a peach house, fernery, vinery and large dog kennels.

Cochrane built the house in 1874. The Cochranes sold the house in 1926 and it was demolished in the following year.

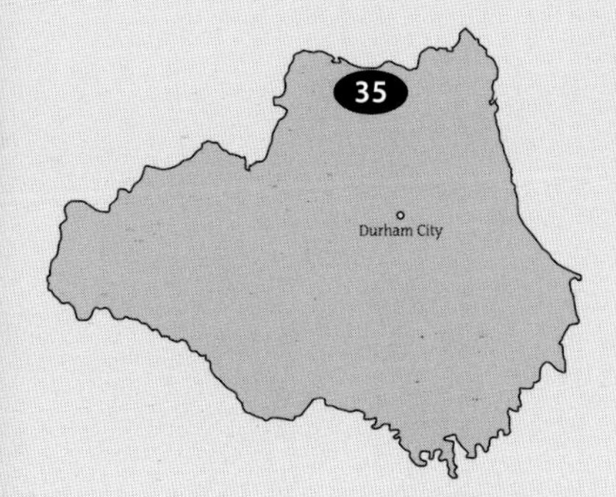

Farnacres

LOBLEY HILL. *c.1180 - 1938*

35

The Farnacres estate was listed in Boldon Book in 1183. In 1429 the estate income was used to establish a Chantry where prayers were offered for the souls of the departed and given into the control of the Bishop of Durham. The Chantry continued until Henry VIII's dissolution when the estate once again passed into private hands. In the early 1600s it was swallowed up by the much grander neighbouring Ravensworth Estate.

The old hall shown on early Ordnance Survey maps, sitting alongside Farnacres, was probably the remaining part of the early Chantry. Bourn's Annals of Whickham Parish tells us that in 1311 the Bishop of Durham wrote to the Dean of Chester that William Lord of Farnacres, Thomas of Holynsyde and certain others acknowledged certain sums of money to be due from them to the Bishop and that they refused to pay. In the fourteenth century it didn't pay to get on the wrong side of the Bishop, although I don't suppose this had any bearing on the fact that Farnacres is demolished and Hollingside a ruin. The site is now covered by the A1 motorway and the buildings of the Team Valley trading estate.

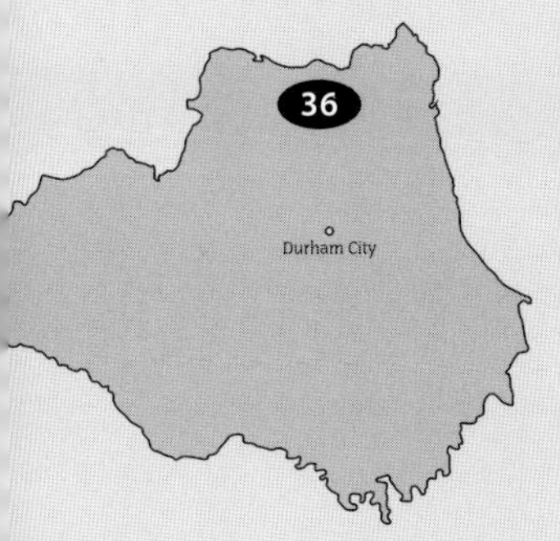

Fell House

LOW FELL. *1807 - 1964*

36

Built in 1807 for Thomas Wilson a local boy made good who worked his way through the ranks to become a partner in the engineering firm of Losh, Wilson and Bell. Wilson is remembered for his Tyneside dialect poetry, in particular 'The Pitman's Pay'. He never forgot his local roots and proved a great benefactor to the poor of Gateshead.

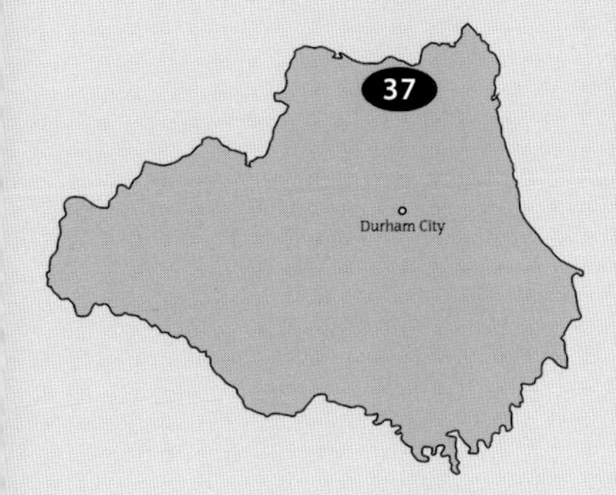

Felling Hall

FELLING. *c.1700 - c.1909*

37

Sir Thomas Surtees became Lord of the Manor of Felling in 1331 and his descendents inherited until 1509. Sir Robert Brandling of Newcastle gained the estate through his marriage to Anne Surtees and it remained in his family until between 1809 and 1850 when the estate was sold in numerous lots.

Surtees tells us in his 'Durham History': *"Felling Hall, an old stone house of which the foundations are now shaken by colliery creeps"*. In 1850 Felling Hall became the Mulberry Inn and circa 1900 was replaced by the current Mulberry Inn.

James the First presented three mulberry trees to the sheriff of Newcastle to encourage silk making in England. One went to Saltwell Hall, one to Axwell Park and the third to Felling Hall, hence the name of the inn.

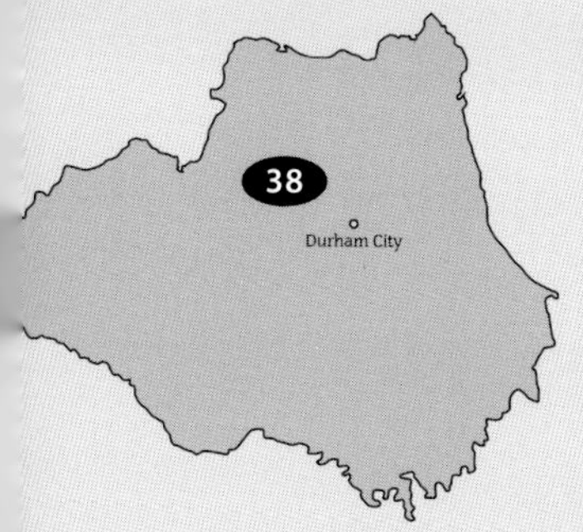

Fen Hall

LANCHESTER. *c.1600*

38

Lanchester Parish was ancient and very extensive, bounded on the north by Ryton, on the west by Stanhope, on the east by Chester-le-Street and on the south by Woolsingham. Previous to Hatfield's survey in 1370 the Ford Estate, now Greenwell Ford, gave names to John de Fenhall and Gamel Del Ford. The early seventeenth century home of the Greenwells is remembered by the coat of arms shown above the doorway of Fen Hall. On its demolition the arms were saved and built into the garden wall of the neighbouring mansion of Greenwell Ford.

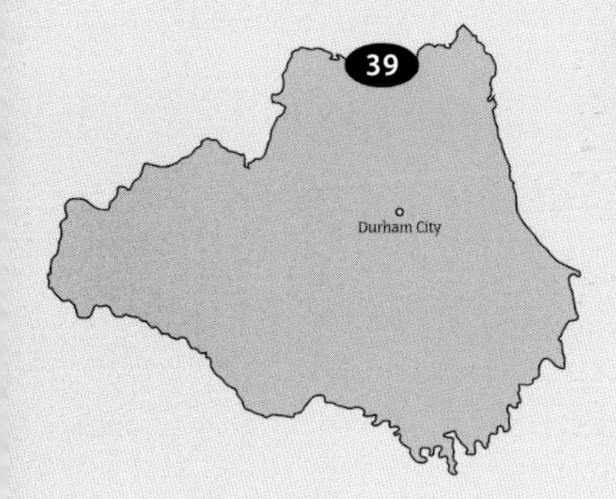

Ferndene

GATESHEAD. *1850s - 1931*

39

Built in the style of neighbouring Saltwell Towers for local rope manufacturer R. S. Newell who built the largest telescope in the world, at the time, in the grounds.

1n 1906 it was leased by nuns to act as a boarding school. In 1911 the school moved to Newcastle and became 'La Sagesse'. The house was demolished in 1931 and the grounds are now covered by housing. The stylish Lodge is a small reminder of Ferndene.

Field House (formerly Enfield House)

GATESHEAD. *1813 -1931*

40

The Field House Estate dated from the 1600s and in 1804 was purchased by George Barras. In 1813 John Dobson designed the new Field House, one of his earliest commisions. In 1895 it became a private boarding school which in 1930 became Gateshead High School. The estate was gradually sold off for building purposes and the house demolished in 1931. The stone from the house was used to build the foundations of the villas of Ferndene and Brighton Roads.

Fishburn Hall

FISHBURN. *c.1690 - 1953*

FISHBURN AND SEDGEFIELD,
IN THE COUNTY OF DURHAM.

Particulars with Plan
OF A
VALUABLE FREEHOLD ESTATE,
(Free of Land Tax, except a Nominal sum),
SITUATE IN THE
Township of Fishburn, and in the Parish of Sedgefield in the County of Durham,
CALLED
"THE FISHBURN ESTATE,"
Consisting of a CAPITAL and COMMODIOUS MESSUAGE and DWELLING HOUSE,
AND
SEVERAL FARM HOUSES AND SUITABLE BUILDINGS,
TWO WELL-ACCUSTOMED INNS, CALLED
THE BEEHIVE & HORSE SHOE INNS,
And 665 Acres, 0 Roods, 26 Perches, more or less, of
EXCELLENT ARABLE, MEADOW, AND PASTURE LAND,
WITH THE VALUABLE SEAMS OF COAL AND OTHER MINERALS THEREUNDER;
AND ALSO OF A FARM KNOWN AS "RYAL HILL,"
SITUATE IN THE TOWNSHIP OF SEDGEFIELD, IN THE COUNTY OF DURHAM,
Consisting of a DWELLING HOUSE, and Out Buildings, and 37 Acres, 3 Roods, 21 Perches, more or less, of Excellent Arable, Meadow, and Pasture Land,
WHICH
WILL BE OFFERED FOR SALE BY AUCTION,
In pursuance of instructions received from the Trustees under the Will of CHRISTOPHER WATKIN, Esq. deceased

BY MESSRS. WATSON & BOWMAN,

AT THE KING'S HEAD HOTEL IN DARLINGTON,
ON TUESDAY, THE 7TH DAY OF OCTOBER, 1873,
AT THREE FOR FOUR O'CLOCK IN THE AFTERNOON PRECISELY.
SUBJECT TO THE CONDITIONS OF SALE TO BE THEN PRODUCED,
In the undermentioned, or such other Lots, as may be decided upon at the time of sale, (if not previously disposed of by Private Contract, of which due notice will be given.)

Applications to view are to be made to JOHN FRIEND, Esq., Fishburn, near Sedgefield, and PARTICULARS with PLAN annexed, and further information can be obtained on application to Messrs. WATSON AND BOWMAN, Auctioneers; Messrs. R. THOMPSON and Co., and MR. ROBERT R. DIXON, Land Agent, all of Darlington; and at the Offices of Messrs. J. W. & C. HUNTON, Solicitors, Richmond, Yorkshire.

41

In 1084 Ranulf De Fissebourne is recorded in a document. In October of 1873 sale particulars tell us: *"The Fishburn Estate consisting of a capital and commodius messuage and dwelling house and several farm houses and suitable buildings."*

Also included with the sale were the Beehive and Horse Shoe Inns, 665 acres of excellent arable, meadow and pasture land, also the farm known as Ryal Hill. In the nineteenth century the hall became a private boys school and in the early twentieth century a store for agricultural produce.

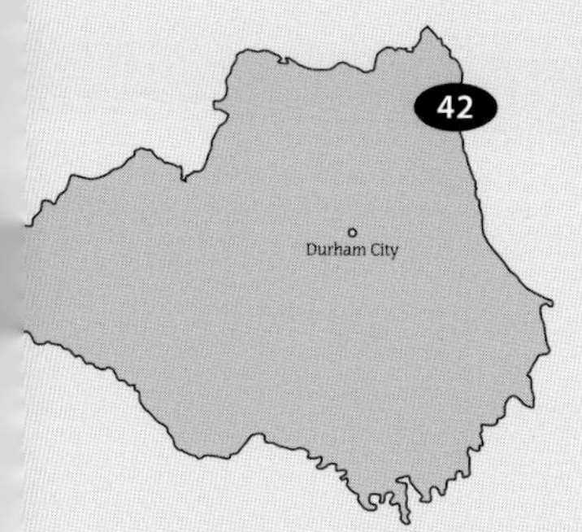

Ford Hall

SUNDERLAND. *1785 - 1929*

42

Built in 1785, by George Mowbray, it was quickly sold to the Goodchild family, Sunderland bankers and landowners. The sale took place in 1791 but the Goodchilds let the house to William Havelock whose son was born there in 1795. This son became General Sir Henry Havelock, hero of the Indian Mutiny who died at Lucknow in 1857. Ford was purchased by Sunderland Council in 1927 and demolished in 1929. It was replaced by the council houses of the Ford estate.

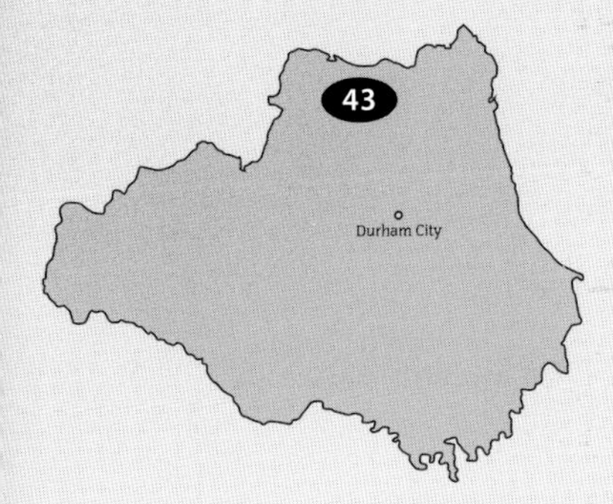

Fugar House

STREET GATE. *c.1300 - 1952*

43

The earliest mention of Fugar House is in 1269 when William De Feugers is granted the twenty-six acre Fugar Estate by the Bishop of Durham. In Bourns Annals of the parish of Whickham we read that Fugar House was one of the free tenancies of the parish of Whickham and gave name to a family. The estate was eventually annexed by the neighbouring Ravensworth Estate. The Ordnance Survey map of 1856 shows Fugar House as part of a large courtyard house. The house was greatly reduced during the next thirty years and became tenemented and was finally demolished in 1952.

The old orchard still contains ancient apple and pear trees. As a boy visiting the Washingwell Woods I used to eat this fruit which was hard and woody but with great flavour.

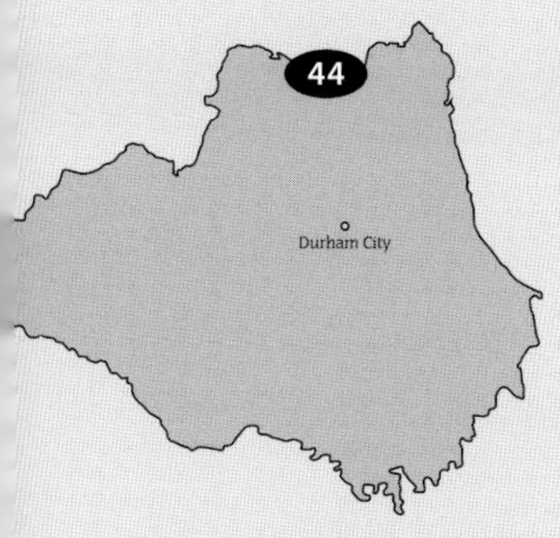

Gateshead Park

GATESHEAD. *Rebuilt 1723 - Enlarged 1730 -33*

44

Originally the Manor House of the Bishop of Durham's park estate. The estate was acquired by William Cotesworth who rebuilt the house in 1723. Sykes local records of 1725 tell us: *"At the Assizes, at Durham, John Brown and Christopher Richardson were tried before Mr. Baron Price for attempting to poison William Cotesworth, Esq., of Park House, Gateshead, their master, by putting arsenic into his chocolate. They were both found guilty. One was Mr. Cotesworth's butler, the other his gardener."*

The house was enlarged in 1730 to the designs of James Gibbs for Cotesworth's son-in-law, Henry Ellison who built Hebburn Hall in 1790. After a serious fire in 1891 the house was turned into a factory. After a second fire the remains of the house were demolished.

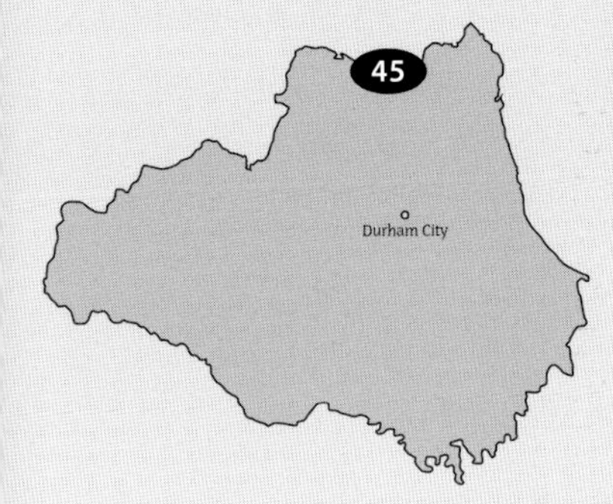

Gateshead Rectory

GATESHEAD. *1825 - 1959/60*

45

The old seventeenth century Rectory of Gateshead stood to the east of the large graveyard surrounding the ancient parish church of St. Mary's. The Rectory was demolished in 1825 and a new one was built in the more desirable suburb of Bensham where new substantial stone terraces and detached villas were appearing. This new Rectory was large and stone built, its quality reflecting the status of the Gateshead Rector in the Diocese of Durham. This house was demolished in 1959/60 and its grounds covered by contemporary housing.

Gibside Hall

ROWLANDS GILL. *1603/20 - altered 1805 - additions 1813/15 - 1856 - shell left*

46

John Sykes' local records of 1866 tells us: *"The mansion House at Gibside, in the County of Durham, was founded by Sir William Blakiston in the reign of King James I."*

Bourn's Annals of Whickham tells us in 1805: "Gibside Hall, after undergoing several important alterations and improvements, was finished and occupied by the Earl of Strathmore." Among the alterations was the removal of a storey from the building, the south front was entirely rebuilt, and a block of offices erected at the east end. Land Girls were billeted in the servants quarters during the first world war.

The grounds are attributed to Lancelot 'Capability' Brown and were planted from 1760 - 70.

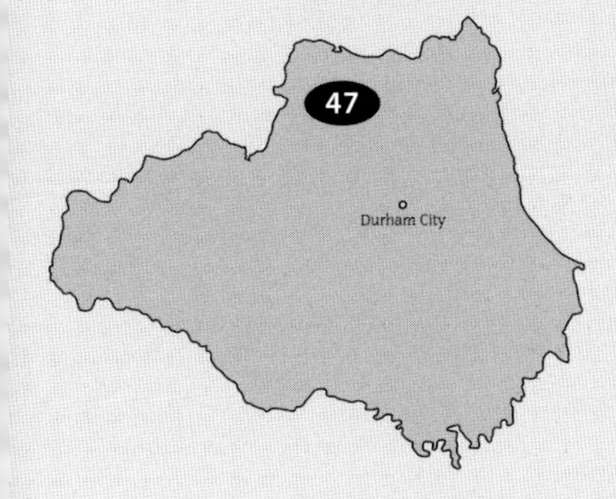

Gibside Orangery

ROWLANDS GILL. *1772/74 - shell remains*

47

Work on quarrying stone for the Orangery began in July 1772. Roof slates were laid that winter with glazing following in the summer of 1773. In 1774 eight ornamental urns were carved to top the facade. Lobbies were placed at both ends of the building to eliminate draughts.

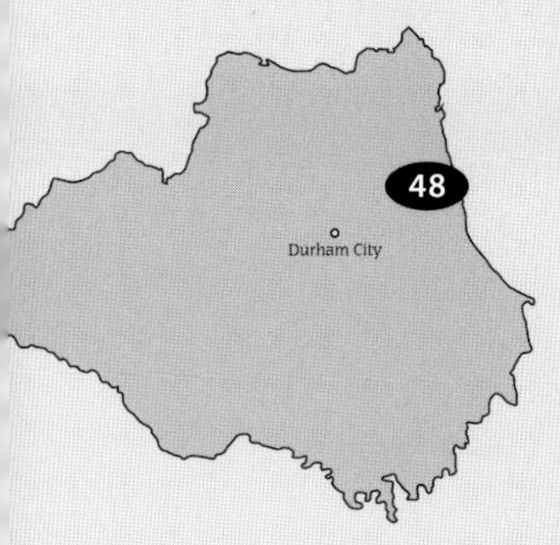

Great Eppleton Old Hall

GREAT EPPLETON.

48

Whellan's Directory of 1894 tells us that: *"Eppleton Old Hall is a plain square building, supposed to have been built in Charles the second's reign, it is now in a state of ruin."*

Eppleton was an ancient manor and formerly home to the Herons in 1391. From them it passed to the Collingwoods and Shadforths and, in 1692, to the Mascalls with who it remained until its demolition at the beginning of the twentieth century. Little Eppleton Hall still survives.

Durham City

49

Greencroft (East and West)

DARLINGTON. *c.1860 - 1970s*

49

All the grandest streets in Darlington seemed to have at least one house owned by the Pease family and Coniscliffe Road was no exception.

Joseph Pease of Southend built Greencroft for his sons Gurney and Edward. When the brothers died the two houses, each with nine bedrooms, were converted into three houses which were demolished in the 1970s.

Greencroft Hall

LANCHESTER. *1670 - C18th additions - 1960*

50

Built by the Clavering family and still belonging to their descendents until demolition, the house was used by soldiers convalescing after the second world war. The eighteenth century stable block was rebuilt as the entrance and Visitors Centre at Beamish museum.

G. A. Cowen in his 'The Braes of Derwent Hunt' says of Greencroft: *"This has been a magnificent sporting property with a delightful house set in a fine position and in lovely surroundings."*

Greencroft Tower Lodge

LANCHESTER. *c.1750 - 1955*

51

This eastern approach to Greencroft Park was known in its early days as the Greencroft Portal. The central gothic arch was flanked by two lodges. Eventual subsidence made the tower unsafe and an estimated repair cost of around four thousand pounds proved to be too expensive. Demolition took place in 1955.

52

Durham City

Greenesfield House

GATESHEAD. - *c.1975*

52

Built in a triangle formed by the junction of Askew Road and Mulgrave Terrace, Greenesfield was purchased from Edmund Graham by Gateshead Council for one thousand, three hundred pounds in 1844 to act as a Town Hall. The building of the Team Valley extension railway, begun in 1867 next to the house, led to the council funding a new Town Hall on Gateshead High Street. This building was restored and replaced by Gateshead Civic Centre, built in the 1980s. Greenesfield was demolished in 1975.

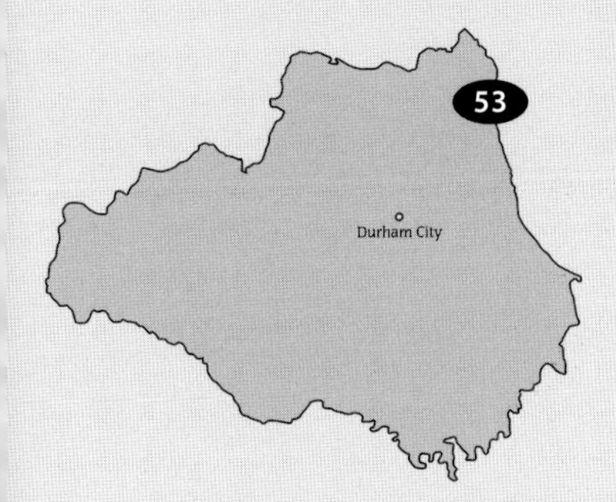

Grindon Old Hall

SUNDERLAND. *c.1580 - 1964*

53

Its long history was unknown until its demolition in 1964 in preparation for the building of the Grindon housing estate. It was hoped that the Old Hall would be converted into a Public House to serve the new housing, but the Cameron's Brewery architects found the building too decayed and it was demolished. It was replaced by a new pub. Ironically a previous owner was Colonel Vaux of the famous Sunderland brewing family. He carried out major improvements and extensions to the Old Hall.

Leo Crangle, in a talk given to the Sunderland Antiquarian Society, said that two Adam Fireplaces from the Old Hall had been bought by Theodore Nicholson, a Sunderland solicitor and a member of the family who became the owners of Vaux Brewery.

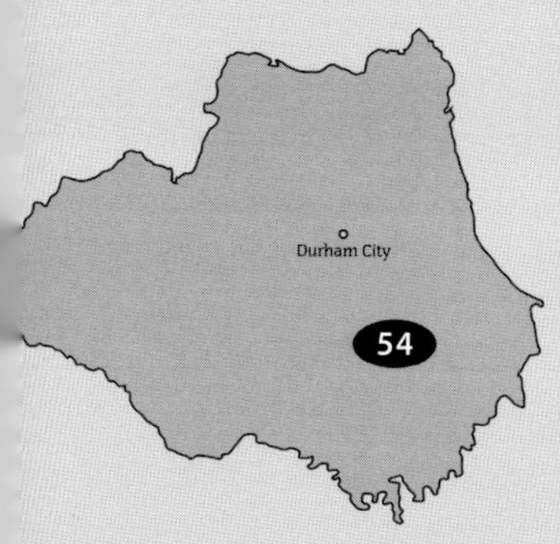

Hardwick Hall - Banqueting House

SEDGEFIELD. *1754 - 57 - 1947*

54

John Burdon bought the Hardwick Estate in 1748 and had James Paine draw up plans for a new house. This was never built and the earlier house still survives and is now a fashionable hotel. Paine was involved in designing or altering several Durham houses, such as Axwell Park, Bradley Hall, Coxhoe Hall, Gibside, Raby and Ravensworth Castle. He also designed a series of garden buildings and ornamental works for Hardwick and these were carried out. These included a doric bath house, temple, grotto and the Banqueting House shown.

All of the buildings suffered vandalism and decay and several of them have been rebuilt or restored. The Banqueting House was beyond repair and can only be remembered by prints, postcards or photographs.

Hartburn Hall

HARTBURN. *1875 - 1930s*

55

Hartburn Village, with its seventeenth and eighteenth century houses and nineteenth century cottages, is called 'very attractive' by the Department of the Environment. Hartburn Hall itself was a later Victorian house with its manicured gardens and lawns surrounded by trees and high walls. The house was demolished in the 1930s and its site is now occupied by the mock Tudor houses of Jesmond Grove. Its two lodges still survive, probably designed by E. E. Clephen who also designed Hartburn Hall - his own house.

Haughton Hall

HAUGHTON LE SKERNE. *C18th - 1981*

56

Haughton Hall was a large double pile eighteenth century house of two storeys and five bays. The entrance front bordered the road through the village and was remarkably plain. The garden front had a double height castellated bow window of three lights at its centre. The house stood near the church on the village green and had a stuccoed finish. In 1894 the house was inhabited by Jonathon Robert Ord Esq., and was replaced by housing in 1981.

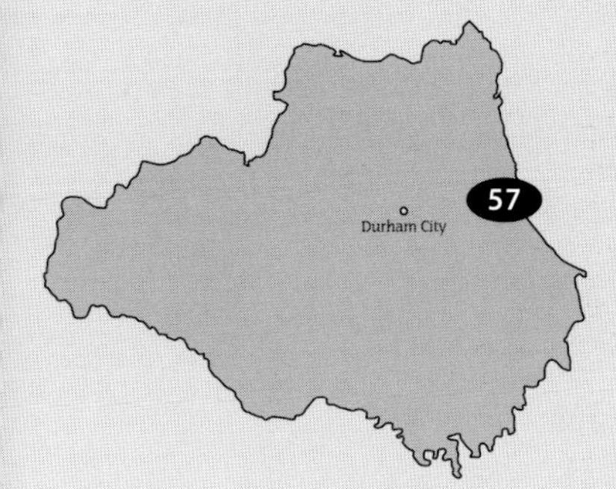

Hawthorn Tower (formerly Hawthorn Hive Cottage, formerly Hawthorn Dene House)

HAWTHORN. *1821 - 1969*

57

Built in 1821 by John Dobson for Major George Anderson and altered in 1850 by Thomas Moore for the Pemberton family of Sunderland. Moore designed Ashbrooke and Low Barnes, the latter also for Richard Pemberton, and both now are lost houses of Sunderland. Hawthorn Tower was home to the Pemberton family from 1836 until 1910 and was a thirty roomed mansion. Hawthorn Halt, a little nearer the coast, was the Pemberton family's private platform where trains would stop for them on demand.

58

Durham City

Heathfield - Summer House

GATESHEAD. *1856 -*

58

Heathfield still survives but is now divided into four luxury apartments. It was one of a number of substantial villas on Durham Road in Gateshead, built mainly for wealthy local industrialists, such as Saltwell Towers, North Dene and Whinney House. This view gives a flavour of the gardens which once surrounded the houses. Large stone lions still guard the drive to Heathfield and its gardens which once had artificial mountains, lakes and an island with a glass pagoda. These, along with the summer house, have all gone with luxury houses built nearby.

Helmington Hall

HUNWICK. *1686 - 1895*

59

A grand nine-bayed house of 1686 with elaborate scrolled pediments over all the windows and front door. Whellan's directory of 1894 tells us: *"Helmington Hall is now in a ruinous state owing to colliery workings."* In the following year fire destroyed what was left of the house. A three bay house is all that remains of Helmington Hall.

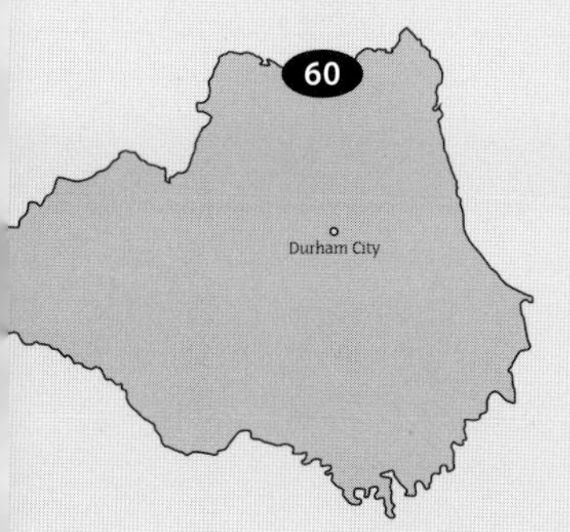

The Hermitage

GATESHEAD. *1870 -1964*

60

The Hermitage was home to William Clark, engineer and co-owner of Clark Chapman Ltd., the great Tyneside engineering company. In 1903 the house became home to High Fell Social Club and continued in this role until demolition in 1964.

The Club continued in a new building on the site until 2014.

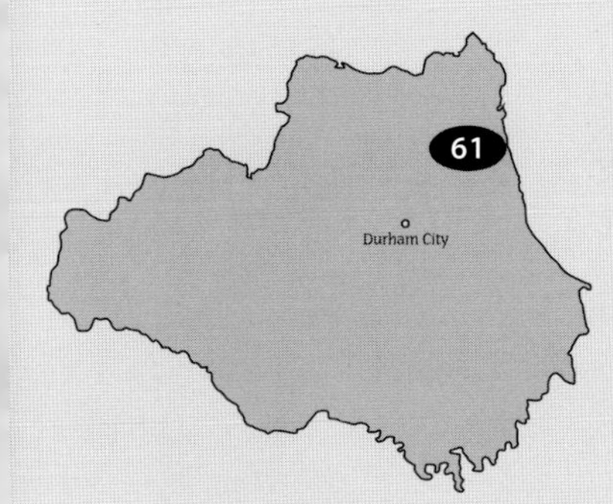

Herrington Hall

MIDDLE HERRINGTON. *c.1570 - 1795 - 1957/58*

61

Herrington was demolished in 1957/58 when cellars dating from circa 1570 were exposed. A house existed from that date until demolition began in 1957. The house was home for several generations of the Robinson family but in 1795 was sold to William Beckwith who built the house shown. A later Beckwith inherited Silksworth House through his wife, Priscilla Hopper, who funded the building of St. Leonard's Church in Silksworth. Herrington passed to the Clay and Moore families and was then bought by the Earl of Durham and occupied by William Lishman Esq., a colliery manager.

In 1947 it was bought by the National Coal Board Miners Welfare Commision with the intention of conversion to a convalescent home. This did not materialise and the house stood empty for several years and gradually deteriorated.

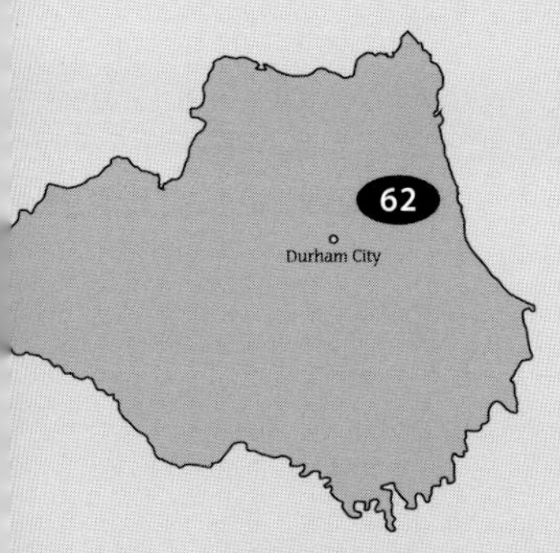

Hetton Hall

HETTON LE HOLE. *Rebuilt 1850 - c.1920*

62

Whellans Directory of 1894 tells us: *"The hall is uninhabited and is fast falling into decay."*

Seat of the Nicholson family and home to Thomas Lyon, 8th Earl of Strathmore and Kinghorne who married the heiress Jean Nicholson. Their son John Lyon, 9th Earl, married Mary Eleanor Bowes of Gibside and Streatlam, the former now a shell and the latter demolished. Hetton and Gibside were only eleven miles apart and John and Eleanor had known each other since childhood.

A later inhabitant of Hetton Hall was Nicholas Wood, chairman of the Hetton Coal Company. He is remembered by having Hetton streets named after his three children, Collingwood, John and Lindsay.

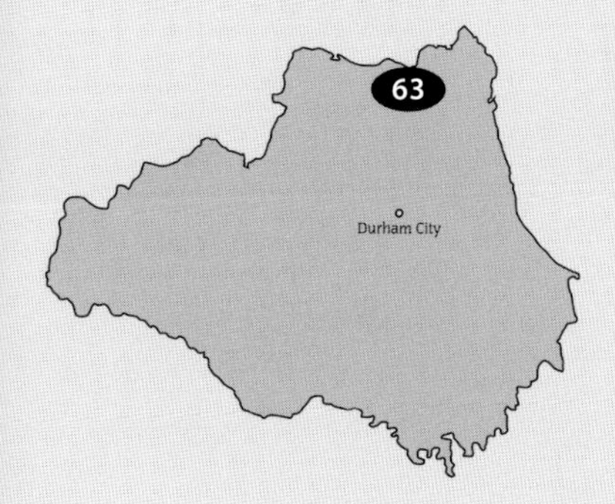

Heworth Rectory

HEWORTH. *1897 - 1975*

63

A ten roomed house built in 1897 to replace the Georgian rectory, which in 1908 became the home to the Heworth, Pelaw, Felling and District Constitutional Club. This Georgian former rectory was demolished itself in 1958 as a casualty of the Felling by-pass road scheme. The 1897 replacement (pictured) was demolished in 1975 during the construction of the transport hub, Heworth Metro Interchange.

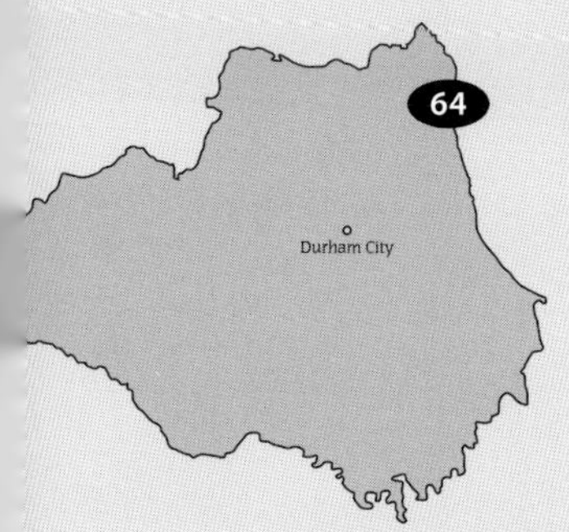

High Barnes

SUNDERLAND. *Rebuilt 1778 - 1900*

64

The Barnes Estate was sold and split in 1668 into two Lots. High Barnes was bought by the Ettrick family and Low Barnes by the Pembertons. The house was demolished in 1900 and replaced by the buildings connected to the Little Sisters of the Poor, who remained there until recent times.

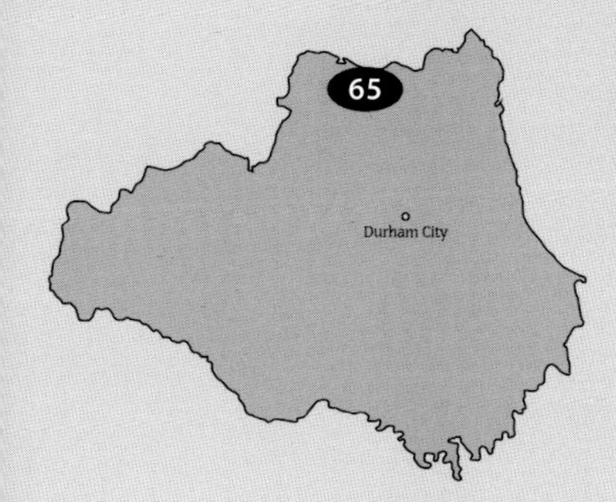

Hollinside

WHICKHAM. *C13th - ruin*

65

At the close of the thirteenth century Hollinside was owned by a family bearing the same name. In 1318 Thomas Hollinside conveyed the manor to William Bointon and from him it passed to the Redheugh family of Gateshead. In 1430 the Harding family took over Hollinside and continued there until 1730. The Hardings were known as the giants of Hollinside because of their unusual height.

The medieval Manor House of the late 1300s was strengthened in the 1400s to counter incursions from Scotland. The house was gentrified at a later date, perhaps when it was bought by the Bowes family from the Hardings and unified into the Gibside Estate. The house suffered a gradual decline into its present ruinous condition. In Whickham churchyard is to be found the tombstone of the last of the Hardings to live at Hollinside. 'Richard Harding, died 22nd August, 1731, aged 76 years.'

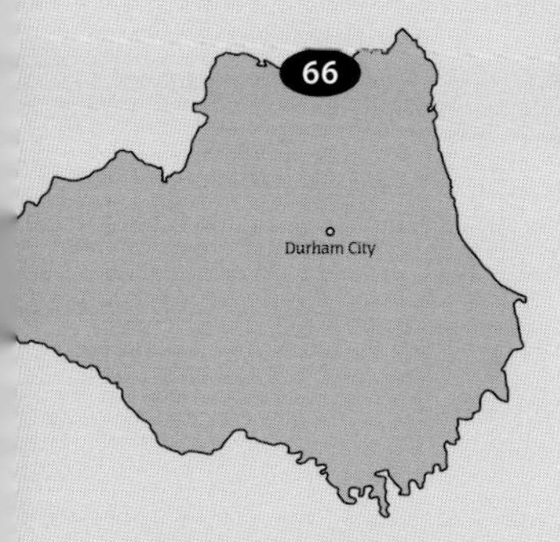

Holly House

GATESHEAD. *C17th - refaced C18th - 1973*

66

Situated on Bensham Road to the west of the Windmill Hills, Holly House was a five bay, three storey, double pile Elizabethan manor house. It was refronted in the 1700s. The house became home to the British Legion, re-founded by Colonel Crouch of the Durham Light Infantry in 1945. The house slowly deteriorated and was demolished in 1973.

Hoppyland Hall

BEDBURN. *Late C16th - burnt and rebuilt 1793 - ruined shell 1952*

67

Syke's local records tell us: "*1793. This month a house, the property of Anthony Leaton, Esq., at Hoppyland, in the county of Durham, was maliciously set on fire and burnt down*".

The house was bought from the Blacketts in 1768 and rebuilt in 1793 by George Leaton Blenkinsopp, staying in his family until the early twentieth century.

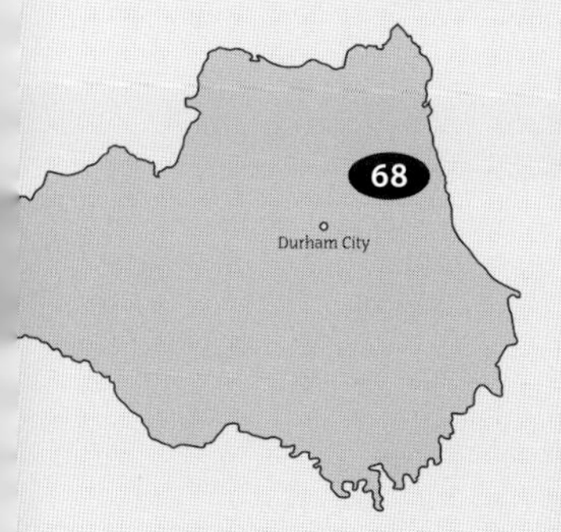

Houghton Grange - Summer House

HOUGHTON LE SPRING.

68

Houghton Grange is now demolished and its site covered by housing. Postcards of the gardens and garden buildings are not that common and this view of the Grange's Summer House, with two maids from the house, shows a typical middle class scene. The staff would wait until the Master and Mistress of the house were out before taking such liberties.

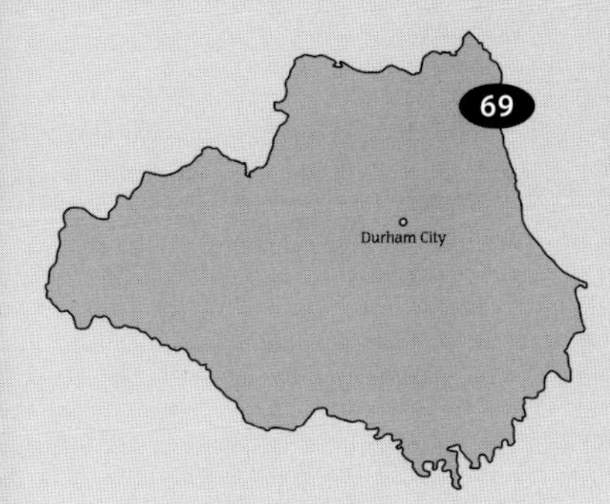

Hylton Castle

SUNDERLAND. *c.1400 - shell*

69

The original tower house of c.1400 still survives and its history records a series of extensions over the centuries. By 1800 the tower had four bay wings of three storeys in height and single storey extensions to the rear. The Hylton family lived at the castle from 1376 until 1746. The castle passed to the Bowes family who sold it in 1862 to William Briggs. He demolished the two wings as well as other additions, taking the castle back to its original dimensions. He also gutted the interior, creating plain and functional accommodation. The castle was then bought by the Monkwearmouth Colliery Company and was gradually reduced to an empty shell.

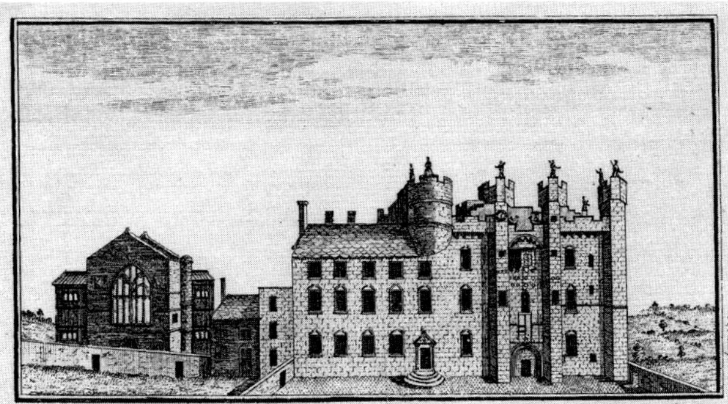

Kibblesworth Old Hall (formerly High Hall, formerly Nether Hall)

KIBBLESWORTH. *c.1720 - 1934*

70

The Newcastle Weekly Chronicle of April 18th, 1874 tells us of the Old Hall having: *"Very insufficient house-room for twelve families of miners beside the village school and one of the two shops in which the community can boast."*

Twenty years later little had changed. Whelans Directory of 1894 says: *"The former residence of the Greenwell family is now let in tenements, part of which is converted into the Post Office, the rest occupied by miners."*

By the time the Old Hall was tenemented in the 1850s, until demolition in 1934, it was known locally as 'The Barracks'.

Lamb Flatt House (later Paradise, later Larchfield)

DARLINGTON. *1811 - 1978*

71

Built as Lamb Flatt House in 1811 for John Backhouse of the Darlington banking dynasty. John was the younger brother of Jonathan of Polam Hall and son of Jonathan of West Lodge, both still standing. For a short time the house was called 'Paradise' but Francis Mewburn, a later owner, renamed it 'Larchfield'. Mewburn was the last borough bailiff of Darlington, the Bishop of Durham's representative in the town. In 1867 Darlington became independent of the Bishop, gaining its municipal charter.

From 1922 until 1975 the house was used as a Catholic Girls Secondary School. It was demolished in 1978 for the building of St. Augustine's Social Centre.

72

Durham City

Lambton Castle

WASHINGTON. *c.1650 -*

72

As can be seen from the before and after postcard views of Lambton Castle, about one third of the house has been removed. The house has a complicated architectural history and includes the old frontage of Harraton Hall which stood here before. The Lambtons bought the Harraton Estate from the Hedworths in 1688 and got local architect Joseph Bonomi to draw plans for a new house which was built in about 1800.

In the 1820s this house was greatly altered by Ignatius Bonomi but the Castle's foundations proved inadequate to support such a large house and subsidence proved a major problem. Bonomi's contemporary, John Dobson, was called in to consolidate the house. In 1862 Dobson's son-in-law, Sydney Smirke was brought in to reconstruct the building.

In 1932 the house had large reductions made but shortly after the Lambton's moved into Biddick Hall, the second house on the estate was often lived in by their agents. The castle is empty but kept in good repair.

The extensive parkland surrounding Lambton Castle, between Washington New Town and Chester-Le-Street, remained largely untouched until recent years. Areas of housing have recently appeared, perhaps a foretaste of things to come.

Landieu (later Norton House)

HARTBURN. - *1970s*

73

Home of Matthias Robinson who opened his first department store in Stockton in 1896. This was followed by a second store in Leeds. His mini empire was bought by Debenhams in 1962. The postcard shows the Robinson family posing in the garden, typical of a Victorian middle-class family with numerous offspring.

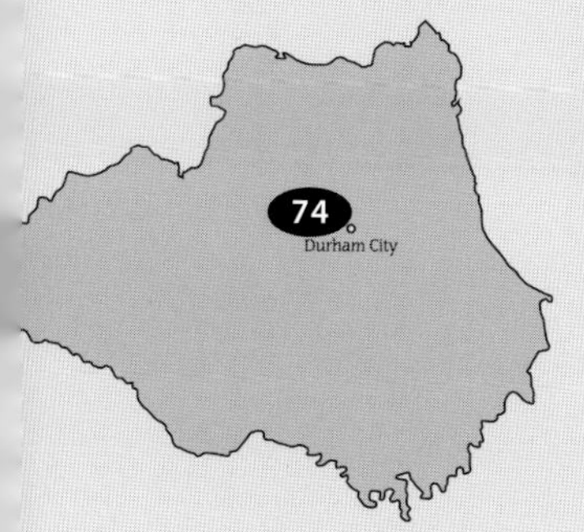

Langley Hall

LANGLEY PARK. *Early C16th - ruin*

74

Only the ruins of the large courtyard house, built by Henry, Lord Scrope, survive. These consist of some high standing walls with several windows and a doorway.

Langton Grange

INGLETON.

75

Whellan's Durham Directory informs us that: *"Langton Grange was for some years occupied by the Dowager Countess of Darlington, afterwards by Captain Watts, and is now the residence of the Trotters"*.

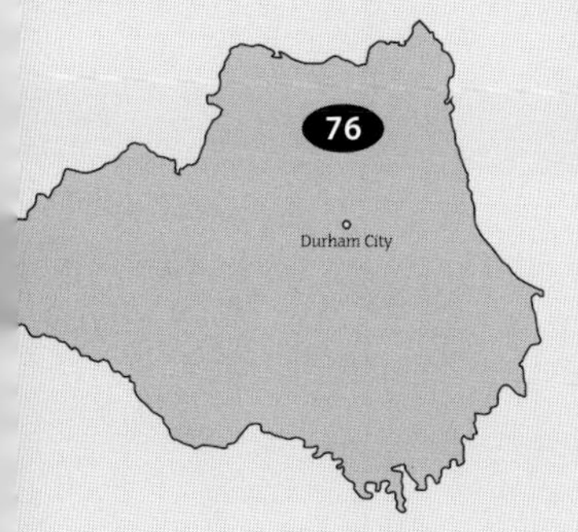

Leafield

BIRTLEY. *c.1870 - 2012*

76

Whellan's Directory of 1894 tells us that: *"There are extensive iron works in this parish, and coal is also worked to a considerable extent in the immediate neighbourhood"*.

The old saying *"Where there's muck there's brass"* obviously applied to Birtley and its grand houses. Birtley Hall, Birtley House, the Old Hall, the Grove, the White House, Vigo House and of course Leafield.

The house was built for Thomas Heppell, chief agent to the Birtley Iron Company and later Pelaw Main Collieries. It was later occupied by Major Ernest Kirkup, mining engineer for Pelaw Mains. Gateshead Urban District Council bought the house for use as a reformatory for boys and it was demolished in 2012.

77

Durham City

Leechmere House (later Leechmere Hall)

SUNDERLAND. - *c.1970*

77

Very early photographs of Leechmere House show a castellated block surrounded by an amazing collection of garden statuary. This was still in place when the house was greatly altered in the 1940s by the National Union of Mineworkers. They turned the house into Leechmere Hall Hostel, a mineworkers convalescent home. The house was demolished circa 1970 to make way for council housing.

Little Usworth Hall

WASHINGTON. *C16th - 1910*

78

Little Usworth Hall was a stone manor house of the sixteenth century with similarities to the tudor house at Tanfield and the old manor house at Newburn in Northumberland, both now demolished. The view above shows the remains of a stone flight of stairs, giving entry at first floor level, and the two and three light windows so typical of the period. The house was demolished circa 1910, being unfit for occupation. The site was covered by terraced housing.

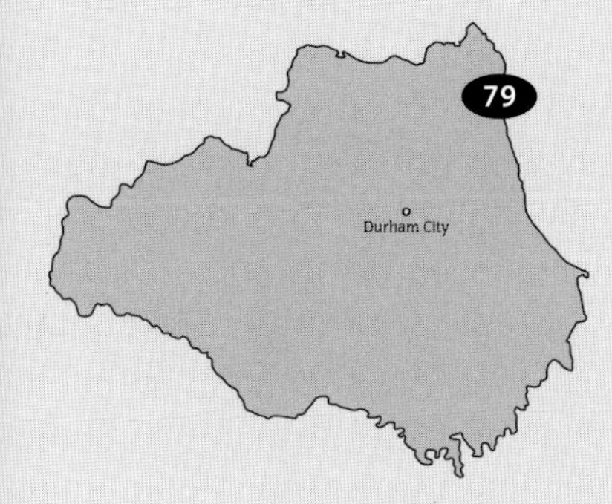

Low Barnes

SUNDERLAND. *Remodelled c.1820 - 1921*

79

Designed by Thomas Moore (1794 - 1869), to replace an earlier house. Moore was described as: "For many years the only architect the town possessed". He also designed the lost Sunderland mansion of Ashbrooke but he is best remembered for his magnificent Monkwearmouth Station.

Low Barnes was built for the Pemberton family in the classical style and had huge grounds including a large garden with "Hot walls and excellent fruit trees". It also had a fish pond stocked with tench and was surrounded by extensive parkland with magnificent specimen trees.

Much of this was kept when the house was demolished in 1921 to form Barnes Park.

Mainsforth Hall

BISHOP MIDDLEHAM. *Rebuilt c.1720 - 1962*

80

Mainsforth was a typical Georgian block of five by four bays, two and a half storeys with a straight parapet. The house was rubble built with a cement render finish. Built circa 1720 by the Surtees family to replace an earlier house owned by the Huttons.

Mainsforth was the birthplace of Robert Surtees (1779 - 1834), famous Durham local historian and friend of Sir Walter Scott and Robert Southey. During the second world war the house was billeted with army officers and later served as a nursing home.

The house was empty from 1953 until demolition in 1962.

Augustus Hare was described as *"A constant guest at all the stately homes of England"*. He described Mainsforth in 1862 as: *"A most pleasant old house, thoroughly unpretending, but roomy and comfortable"*.

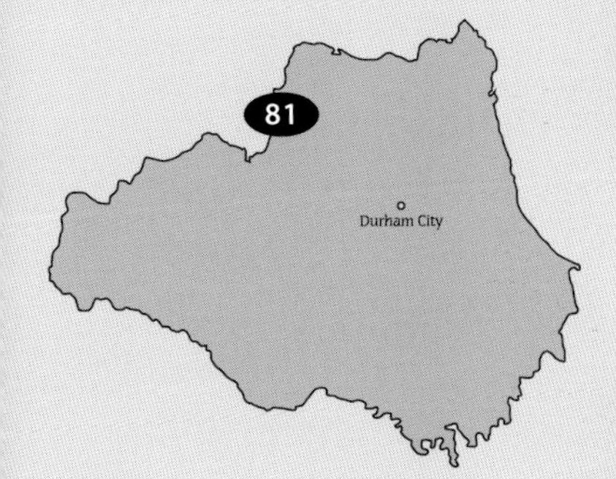

Medomsley Hall

MEDOMSLEY. *c.1730 -*

81

In the late nineteenth century Medomsley Hall and Medomsley Manor House were both owned by the Hunter family. They replaced the Manor House in 1890 with a new house which still stands today. By this time the hall had for many years been used as the Vicarage. The 1894 Directory shows that Canon Cockin M.A. was living at the Vicarage. William Hedley, mining engineer at Consett, was the occupant of the recently rebuilt Manor House.

The first view shows the fine front of the hall with its curious attic built into the eaves. The Hall was very like Newhouse, Sir Walter Blacketts grand house at Ireshopeburn in Weardale, built in 1732. The second view shows the large Georgian wing added to the rear of the house. Although placed at the centre of the village the Hall was surrounded by large, well wooded grounds and manicured lawns.

Moor House

WEST RAINTON. *1840 -*

82

Designed by John Dobson in 1840 for John Dunn Esq. Poor old Mr. Dunn didn't live to enjoy his new house for long. The sale plans of February 1843 say that *"Moor House, late the property of John Dunn Esq., deceased."* The house was sold by Messers. Small and Brough at the Waterloo Hotel in Durham. The estate was advertised as being around one hundred acres and stated that: *"The hind will show the farm and outbuildings, upon application on the estate, and the house may be viewed on the Monday in each week, between the hours of ten and four o'clock."*

The plans also show the route of the proposed line of the railway from Darlington to Newcastle passing just to the west of the house. Perhaps another reason for the sale.

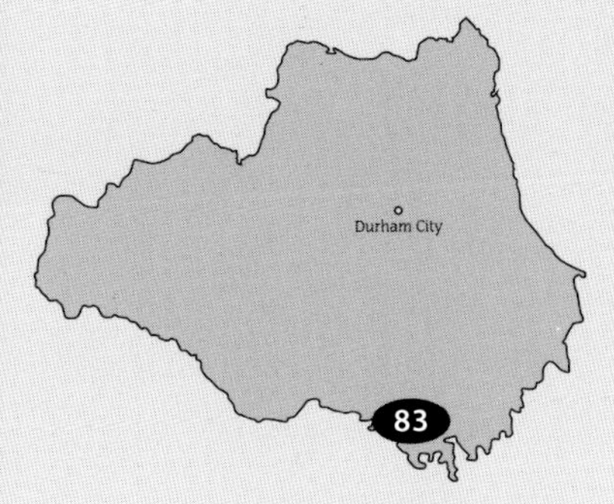

The Mount

DARLINGTON. *Early C19th - 1925*

83

The Mount stood on the spot where Highbury Road meets Carmel Road. From the 1860s until the beginning of the first world war the house became a boarding school for young ladies, run by Miss Fearnley and Miss Woodward. Many medium sized houses became home to small schools run by spinsters living under reduced circumstances. The money made from schooling a few young ladies helped them live in genteel poverty. The house continued as a boarding school until 1914 and was demolished in the 1920s.

Neasham Hall

NEASHAM. *C18th - (extended 1834 - 37) - 1970*

84

The original eighteenth century home of the Blacketts and Turners was bought by Colonel Cookson who commissioned John Dobson to extend the hall in 1834. Dibson added two large wings to the house between 1834 and 1837. The house was demolished in 1970 and replaced by a smaller house designed by Sir Martyn Beckett in 1971. Beckett paid homage to the eighteenth century Neasham by building two semi-circular bays on the main front using some architectural fragments from the original house.

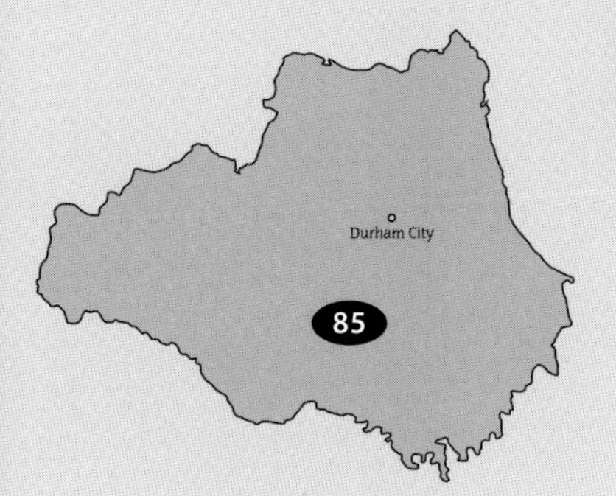

Newton Cap Hall

BISHOP AUCKLAND. *c.1750 - ruinous 1834 - 1868/70*

Old Newton Cap Hall. Bishop Auckland.

85

Whellan's Directory of 1894 tells us that the last of the Bacon family of seventeenth century Newton Cap Old Hall: *"Commenced building a stately hall here, now in ruins, is stated to have led a profligate life, squandering his property in extravagance and gaming, and at length terminating his existence by suicide in his unfinished mansion."*

The new hall was never finished and both halls were declared *"for some years in a state of rapid decay."* Both halls ended up in the hands of Newton Cap Colliery and were demolished in 1868 and 1870. The stone pilasters and brick walls are reminiscent of Newton Hall in Durham city, also demolished.

86

Newton Hall

DURHAM. *1717 - 1926*

86

Newton Hall was a stately, brick built, seven bay house of two and a half storeys. The main front was enlivened by a three bay applied, shallow portico of stone supporting a frieze and portico which ended below the half storey roofline. Rainwater heads were dated 1751 but perhaps the half storey was added to the house at a later date. Newton was built for the Liddells of Ravensworth and later became home to the Russells of Brancepeth.

By the late eighteen hundreds the house became the Durham county lunatic asylum. During the first world war it housed soldiers. Army occupation often sounded the death knell for many country houses and Newton Hall proved to be no exception. After a period of decay the house was demolished in 1926. Its name is remembered by the Newton Hall housing estate which covers the site. The owner of the estate in 1879 was Anthony Lax Maynard J.P.

North Biddick Hall (later Cook's Hall)

WASHINGTON. *C16th - 1966*

87

The north wing of the Hall dated in large part from the sixteenth century, but the site is recorded as being inhabited from the thirteenth. Locally the house was better known as Cook's Hall after Joseph Cook, founder of the Washington Iron Works, whose home it was. After suffering subsidence problems the Hall was demolished in 1966 by Washington Development Corporation for the building of Washington New Town.

Norton House

NORTON. *c.1730 - 1934*

88

Pevsner tells us that Norton Village: *"is still the finest in the county, at least in the eyes of those who like their villages wealthy."* Norton village green still lives up to this description. Norton House was one of three grand houses built facing the green, Norton Hall and the Red House still survive but Norton House was demolished in 1934. The house had long been home to the Hogg family who had the two wings added to the original eighteenth century house, in the mid nineteenth century.

Number 8, Hall Terrace

GATESHEAD. *c.1830 - 1970s*

89

Neville Whittaker in his 'Old Halls and Manor Houses of Durham' says: "*Terrace houses of the middle classes produced in towns like Hartlepool, Sunderland and Durham are as fine as any of this type to be found in these islands.*" He could easily have included the Gateshead suburb of Bensham in this list. Hall Terrace was one of the earliest of these terraces, closely followed by Walker and Regent Terraces - Walker Terrace formed of five bay houses.

Number 8 Hall Terrace was home to the Ord family from 1901 until 1939. The picture shows Alice Jane Dance Ord relaxing at her front door. The family group includes her children Bertram Thomas and Helen May on the front steps. The view of the dining room shows a typical middle class home of the time.

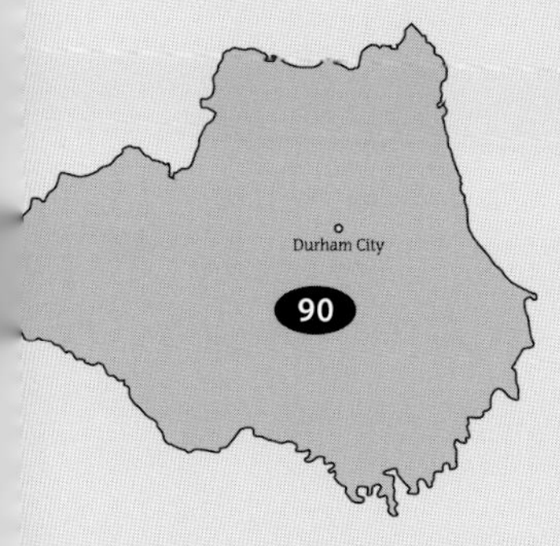

Old Park Hall

BYERS GREEN. *c.1760 enlarged - 1901*

90

Whellan's Directory of 1894 tells us: *"Old Park House or Hall occupies a beautiful and retired situation, about a mile above the Wear, and not far from Byers Green station. It is an interesting old hall, with many attractive architectural features, and has at some time been the residence of some family of note. It is a spacious and well built house, at present occupied as a farmhouse."*

The house had been enlarged in the 1760s by the Wharton family who had also added the 'attractive architectural features' mentioned. Old Park was the seat of the Wharton family from circa 1750 until 1868 when they sold it to the Church Commissioners who demolished the house in 1901.

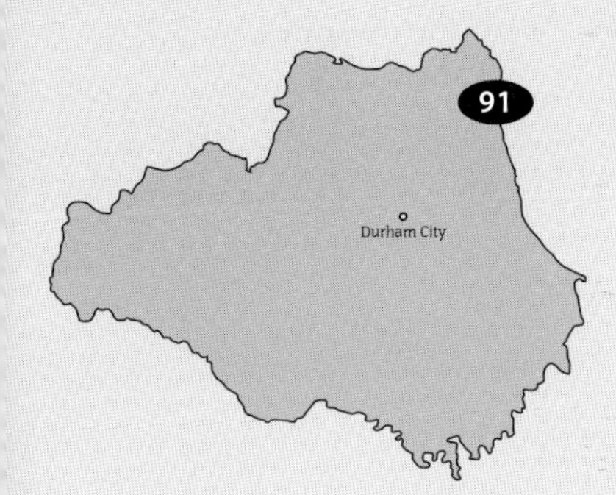

Pallion Hall

SUNDERLAND. *C13th - 1790 - 1901*

91

It's a huge leap of imagination to picture a vinery, peach house and beautiful riverside gardens on land that was to become Sunderland's most industrialised area. This was the idyllic situation of Pallion Hall before it was replaced by the Coles Cranes factory.

There was a hall here in the thirteenth century which passed from the Daldon family to the Bowes. They in turn sold it in 1572 to the Goodchilds of Ryhope Hall who, in 1790, built the hall pictured above.

Pallion's claim to fame is as the birthplace of Sir Joseph Wilson Swan, inventor of the incandescent light bulb. Swan spent the rest of his life at Underhill in Low Fell.

Durham City

92

Parkhead Hall (formerly Derwent Villa)

WINLATON. *1823 - 1910*

92

Parkhead Hall was built by George Heppel Ramsay J.P., who lived there until his death in 1879. Ramsay was a successful owner of coal mines, manufacturer and land agent. His eldest daughter Margaret married Charles John Reed, a co-founder of Newcastle breweries, in 1890.

The hall passed to Ramsay's grandson, George Robinson Ramsay, then to his son John Taylor Ramsay who died there in 1910. The house was then sold to a mining company who demolished it in that same year.

The beautiful view overlooking Axwell Park estate is little changed. The Ramsays also owned Ebchester Hall and its estate, farther up the Derwent valley.

Pelton Vicarage

PELTON. *1845 - 1986*

93

Pelton Vicarage was built at a cost of £1,083 and one shilling in 1845 and paid for by subscriptions from local land owners and colliery owners. The house was large enough to house the vicar and family, a curate and servants and came complete with stables. The Vicarage was demolished in 1986 and the site is now occupied by Pelton Grange Nursing Home.

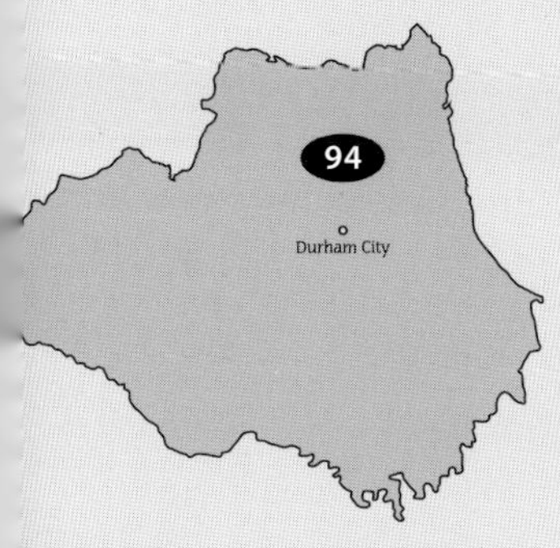

Prospect House

CHESTER-LE-STREET. *1859 - 1902*

94

Built for George Murray in 1859 and originally with a garden with an ornate fountain in front. The house was bought by the Primitive Methodists in 1882 and was demolished in 1902 and the Central Methodist Church built on the site. The gardens are now covered by roads.

Ravensworth Castle

LAMESLEY. *C12th built - 1724 - altered 1754 - 1808 - 1840 - 1952/53*

Pevsner called Ravensworth:
"The most splendid and most picturesque monument of the romantic medieval revival."

The castle was built in the twelfth century and an eight hundred acre park enclosed by licence by Richard II, circa 1390. The house was bought by Thomas Liddell, Newcastle alderman, and his wife Barbara Strangeways. The castle was altered by James Paine in 1754 but Sykes tells us that in 1808: *"This year, nearly the whole of the old castle of Ravensworth, Durham, was taken down, and the present splendid mansion was begun on a beautiful gothic plan furnished by Nash."*

In 1920 an extensive sale of furniture, books and art treasures was held and the family moved to Eslington in Northumberland. After use as a private school, the castle was largely dismantled in 1952. Despite sitting alongside the A1 motorway, the park is remarkably intact.

RAVENSWORTH CASTLE NORTH VIEW GATESHEAD

COURTYARD OF RAVENSWORTH CASTLE GATESHEAD

Stableyard, Ravensworth Castle. (192)

RAVENSWORTH CASTLE WESTVIEW GATESHEAD

96

Durham City

Ravensworth Castle - Alms Houses

LAMESLEY. *1835 - 1967*

96

The Lady Ravensworth Alms Houses were built and endowed by Maria Susannah in 1835. They were to house eight 'poor and aged females' and had a dedication inscription which read: *"Anno Domini MDCCCXXXV. These Alms Houses were built by Maria Susannah Ravensworth in memory of her two departed children. It is good for me that I have been afflicted that I might learn Thy statutes. CXIX Psalm, IXXI verse."*

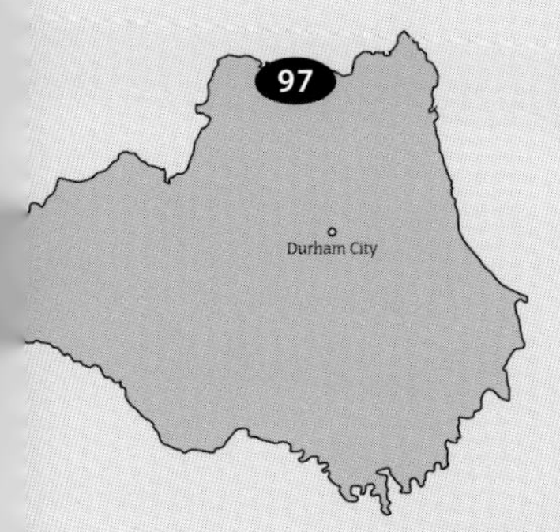

Ravensworth Cottage

DUNSTON. *c.1710 - 1969*

97

This is Mr. William Richard Poole, standing proudly in front of his cottage on his daughter's wedding day. The cottage had an irregular rear and a re-fronted Georgian facade of four bays.

An advert of May 1869 tells us: *"Ravensworth Cottage - To be Let with entry first week in June, an excellent house at Dunston known as 'Ravensworth Cottage'. Containing dining room, drawing room and breakfast room, four bedrooms, two large kitchens, store room, two cellars, an excellent pantry etc. There is a covered in yard, with coach house and large and small greenhouses attached. Gas and water laid into the house. A large flower garden in front, with an excellent kitchen garden. The house is within easy distance of Newcastle and very conveniently situated for parties having business in town who desire to live in the country."*

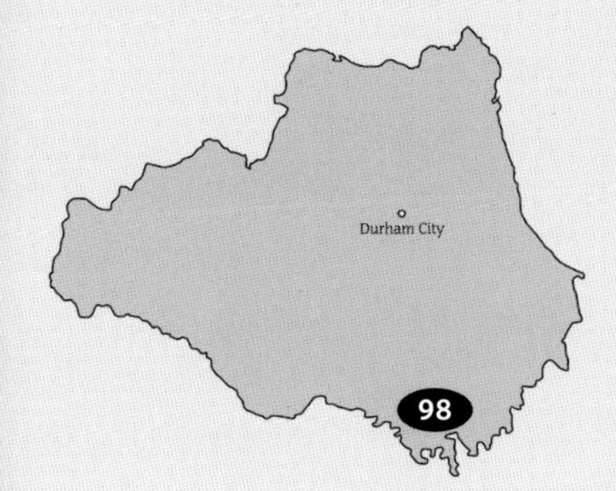

Red Hall

HAUGHTON-LE-SKERNE. *1830 - 1984*

98

The Red Hall estate was bought by Robert Colling in 1697 and stayed in the family's possession for the next two hundred years. In later years the Colling family became widely known as cattle breeders and their prized stock was used to improve herds throughout the country. The money raised from these sales enabled the Collings to live very comfortable lives and, during the nineteenth century, the various family members lived in Monkend Hall, Barmton, Ely Hill, Skerningham and Ketton Hall.

The replacement Red Hall built in 1830 was designed by Philip Wyatt, youngest son of the nationally known architect James Wyatt. The Tudor gothic house, designed by Philip, was bought by Darlington Council in 1965 and, after deterioration, was demolished by them in 1984.

Redheugh Hall

GATESHEAD. *c.1280 - 1936*

99

A Charter of 1280 states that the manor house and estate of Redheugh are owned by Alexander Del Redheugh. The estate passed to the Liddells of Ravensworth, to the Earls of Derwentwater and, in 1748, was conveyed to the Askew family. they held the estate until its break up in the 1880s. The estate had begun to deteriorate long before this. The enclosure commissioner Thomas Bell said of Redheugh in 1838: *"I consider the mansion house is destroyed as the residence of a gentleman and the estate greatly lessened in value."*

In 1850 the estate was offered for sale for building land as it was: *"No longer suitable as a gentleman's residence."* The Redheugh Colliery Company were the last owners and let the house to Wilkinson's Mineral Water Company. The site was covered by terraced houses, demolished to make way for 1960s apartments - now also being demolished.

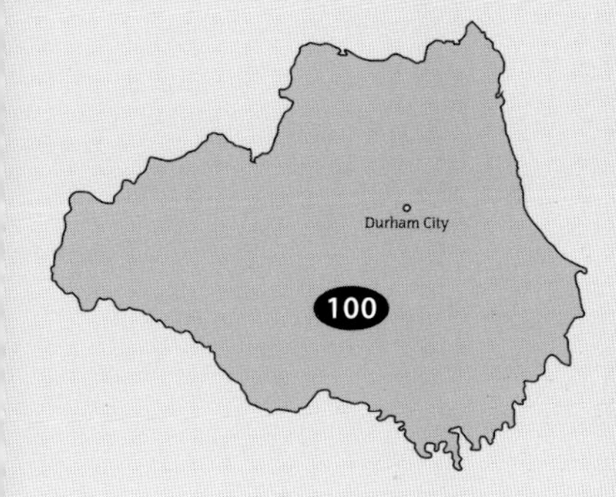

Red House

HIGH ETHERLEY. - *1949*

100

Red House was home to the Stobart family until it was turned into a hospital for soldiers at the beginning of the first world war. During the second world war troops were billeted in the house which had suffered during army occupation. The house was demolished in 1949 and housing now covers the site.

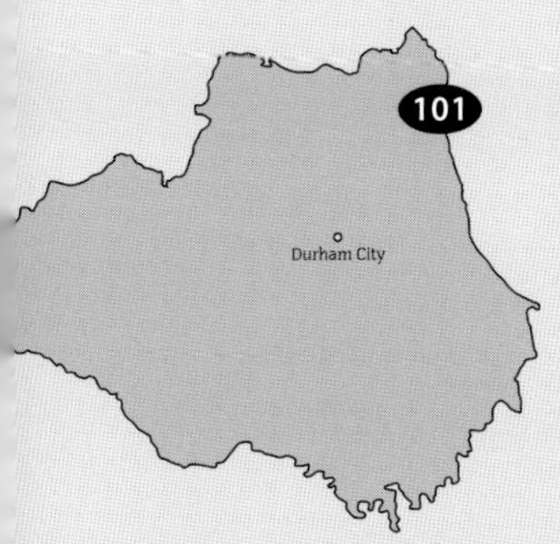

Ryhope Hall

SUNDERLAND. *c.1600 - 1960s*

101

Leo Crangle's article on the old houses of Sunderland says of Ryhope Hall: *"This Hall had long rambling passages, arched doorways, leaded windows and ancient fireplaces."*
The stable block, in later years, was converted into houses known as 'Robson's Place' and the tower added later to the house as 'Robson's Folly'. Above the front door was placed the arms of the Booth family, three boars' heads erect.

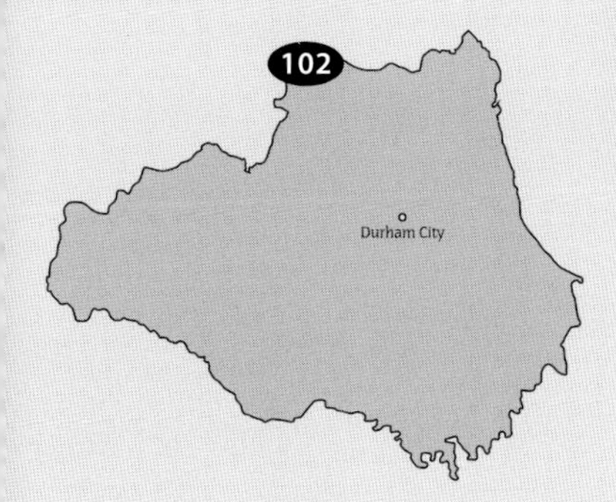

Ryton House

RYTON. *c.1720 - c.1960*

102

Ryton was a brick built house of the early eighteenth century with a curious design. The entrance front was of five bays and two storeys, whilst the side was of six bays and three storeys. Unfortunately the postcard view shown does not show how the internal layout functioned.

The demolished stable block, just yards from the house, was built in eighteenth century gothic style and was paralleled by the stables at Blaydon House, almost twins. The Blaydon stables were demolished in late 2020.

Ryton House throughout its life was home to the Humble family, coal owners and horse breeders and then, through marriage, to the Lambs. The Humble family was well known in Tynedale for its support of the local hunts.

103

Durham City

Saltwell Hall

GATESHEAD. *Late C16th - altered C18th - 1936*

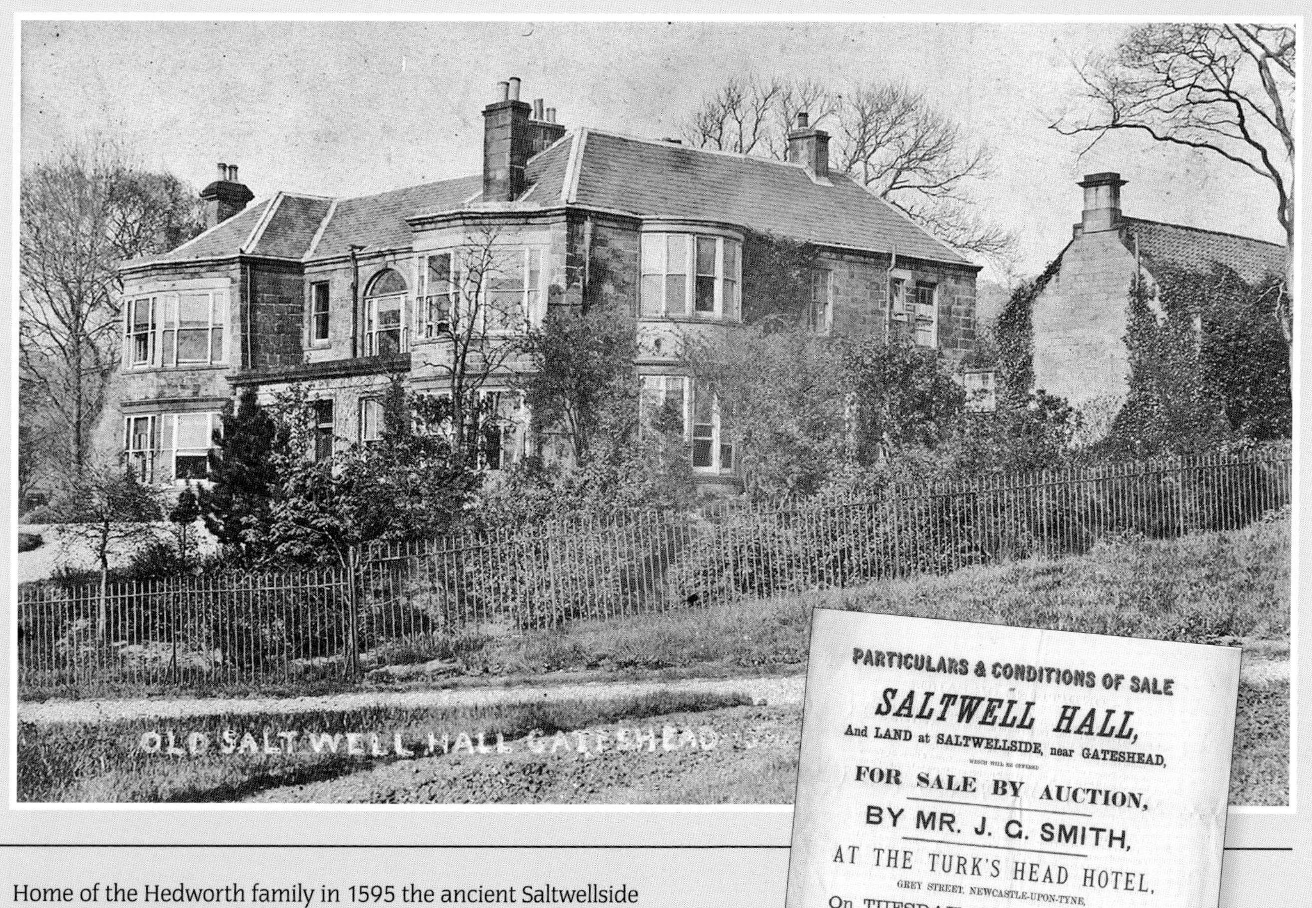

PARTICULARS & CONDITIONS OF SALE

SALTWELL HALL,

And LAND at SALTWELLSIDE, near GATESHEAD,

WHICH WILL BE OFFERED

FOR SALE BY AUCTION,

BY MR. J. G. SMITH,

AT THE TURK'S HEAD HOTEL,

GREY STREET, NEWCASTLE-UPON-TYNE,

On TUESDAY, MARCH 26th, 1878,

AT THREE O'CLOCK IN THE AFTERNOON PRECISELY.

IF NOT SOLD, THE PROPERTY WILL BE OFFERED IN TWO LOTS.

PARTICULARS.

All that valuable Freehold Estate of Saltwellside, near Gateshead, in the County of Durham, comprising the Mansion House known as "Saltwell Hall," the Shrubberies, Greenhouses, Stabling, Coach Houses, Gardener's Cottage, Lodge, Farm House and Buildings, with the Arable and Pasture Lands attached, in the occupation of W. M. Angus, Esq., and others, the whole containing an area of 113A. 0R. 21¼P. more or less.

If not Sold in One Lot it will be offered as follows:—

Lot 1.—The Mansion House, Shrubberies, Greenhouses, Stabling, Coach Houses, Gardener's Cottage, Lodge, Farm House, and Buildings, with the Land extending from Saltwell Lane to the Team Valley Railway, and containing an area of 42A. 3R. 24¾P. more or less.

Lot 2.—The Land extending from the Team Valley Railway partly to the river Team and partly to the Mill Race, bounded on the North by Land belonging to the Representatives of W. W. Burdon, Esq., deceased, and on the South by Land belonging to Lord Ravensworth, and containing an area of 70A. 0R. 35¾P. more or less.

The Purchaser of Lot 2 shall have a Right of Way over and along a road 20 feet wide on the Northern Boundary of Lot 1, and extending from Saltwell Lane to the Archway through the Railway Embankment, the centre of which road shall be in a straight line between a point 10 feet from the inside of the Wall at the North-Eastern corner of Lot 1 to the centre of the said Archway. The road shall be made and maintained at the joint expense of the Purchasers of both Lots.

The mines of coal within and under the property do not belong to the Vendor, and are excepted from the sale, with such liberties and powers in relation thereto as the Owner or Owners of the excepted premises is or are entitled to.

103

Home of the Hedworth family in 1595 the ancient Saltwellside estate was named after the medieval 'Salte Welle' in Saltwell Road with its grand canopy rebuilt in 1872. The Hall was at the centre of the estate which was largely sold in 1903. The land is now covered by Saltwell Park, Saltwell Cemetery and the Team Valley Trading Estate. The Hall was later used as an isolation hospital before demolition in 1936.

One of the three mulberry trees presented by James the first to the area went to Saltwell Hall. It is claimed that it was blown down in 1917.

Seaton Carew Vicarage

SEATON CAREW. *1833 - 1970s*

104

The parsonage of Seaton Carew was built for the Reverend A. Guinness in 1833 in Tudor style. The house cost seven hundred pounds to build, which was relatively inexpensive compared to similar commissions. Anthony Salvin designed the parsonage. He was a member of the family whose seat was Croxdale Hall in Durham. They have lived at Croxdale since the fourteen hundreds and are still there today.

Sherburn Hall

SHERBURN. *C16th - C20th*

105

Home to the Pearson family in the sixteenth century, Sherburn passed to the Tempests, the Mowbrays and the Hoppers. In 1827 it became home to the Pembertons of Sunderland. Finally the house passed to T. C. Thompson Esq. The reading room and library, which was established in 1850 in Sherburn, was generously supported by Mr. Thompson. Many Durham villages had reading rooms, libraries or perhaps both, who owed their existence to the local Estate owners, often mine owners or managers. They supported self education and were an integral part of the early Labour movement in the Durham coalfield.

106

Durham City

Sherburn Tower

ROWLANDS GILL. *C19th - C20th*

106

Often used to house the managers of the local colliery, the size and stylish adornment of Sherburn Tower reflect the importance of these individuals in the north east economy. Many of the larger landowners relied greatly on their agents and mine managers to keep the Estate wheels turning to provide huge revenues that enabled them to live in such grand style. With the owners providing mining villages, shops and reading rooms the managers had huge autonomy in hiring and firing, rent collection and social events. As long as the money kept rolling in the owners were happy.

107

Durham City

Sheriff Hill Hall

GATESHEAD. *1823/24 - 1967*

107

Designed by John Dobson for Newcastle businessman Matthew Plummer, who together chose the site for the house with its amazing views of the Tyne and River Team valleys. It sat at the top of Sheriff Hill, named after the ancient custom of the Sheriff of Newcastle meeting the Judges coming to sit in Newcastle, and escorting them and their retinues into the town.

The house was built to a very similar design that Dobson used at Benwell House, also now demolished, in Newcastle. Plummer, the new owner, had masterminded the development of the Newcastle to Carlisle Railway and became chairman of that company. The house was converted into Gateshead High School in the 1940s until 1963 and was demolished by Gateshead Council in 1967. The servants' wing survived, having been converted into a house in 1925.

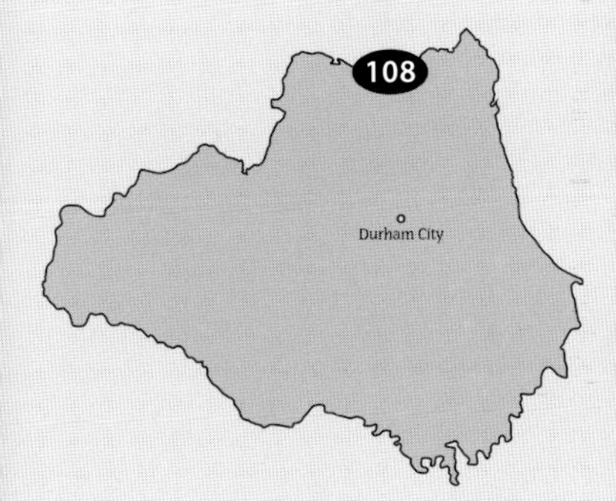

Shipcote House

GATESHEAD. - *1931*

108

Helen May Ord posing in front of her uncle's residence, Shipcote House. The house was home to a succession of notable Gateshead glass makers and designers. In 1841 it was home to George Sowerby, glass maker, and his daughter Githa, later to become a well known book illustrator and playwright. In the 1870s it was occupied by the Strang family. Thomas Rankin Strang married a daughter of William Wailes, the famous designer and maker of stained glass windows which can be found today in churches in the United Kingdom and abroad.

In 1920 the house lost its domestic role, becoming Gateshead and District Trades Union Hall Social Club until its demolition in 1931. The house and its grounds were replaced by Shipcote swimming pool and Gateshead central library and car park.

Durham City

109

Snotterton Hall

SNOTTERTON.

109

Snotterton, near Staindrop, was anciently a manor and part of Staindropshire gifted to the Shrine of St. Cuthbert by King Canute. Known as Cnapaton, the site of the Hall is occupied by Snotterton Hall Farm, formerley known as Raby Grange built in 1831. The gable end of the view above shows signs that a large building was once attached. Could the building shown be a surviving 'service wing' once part of the original Snotterton Hall?

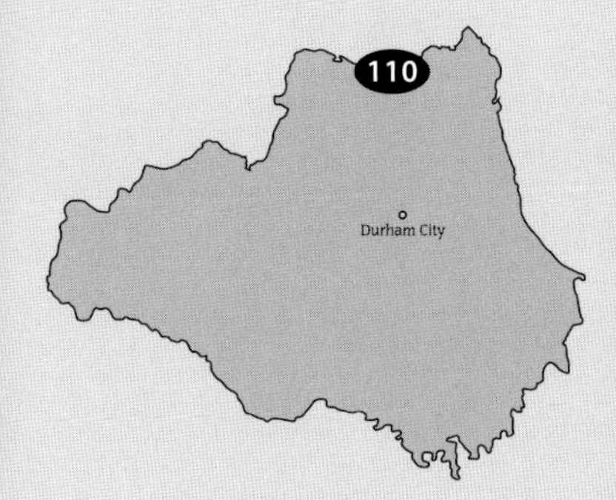

South Dene Tower

GATESHEAD. *c.1851 - 1956*

110

The many grand villas of Durham Road and Saltwell Road were often home to Tyneside industrialists. South Dene Tower was home to James Redmayne, a director of Felling Chemical Company and later to J. Ford Maling, owner of the Maling Pottery in Byker, Newcastle. The house was turned into apartments before demolition in 1956. The entrance gates survive and are now used as the exit to Saltwell Crematorium which was built on the site. Many of the planting and trees of the old gardens survive.

South Dene is very similar to neighbouring Saltwell Towers built by William Wailes in 1860 - 1871. Being much smaller it has been suggested that South Dene was built as a model for the much larger Saltwell Towers.

South Hetton Hall

SOUTH HETTON. *c.1830 - 1974.*

111

Whellan's Directory of 1894 tells us that: "*South Hetton is a considerable village, containing about five hundred houses, almost entirely occupied by miners.*" It is therefore no surprise to discover that the occupant of the Hall at that time is Wiliam Outerrson Wood Esq., chief agent to South Hetton Coal Company Ltd. The Hall later became the headquarters of that company. Wood was from a family of agents and colliery managers who lived for relatively short periods of time in houses like South Hetton and then moved on to collieries new. The house later was used as a remand home and the site is now covered by South Hetton Industrial Estate, on Hall Street.

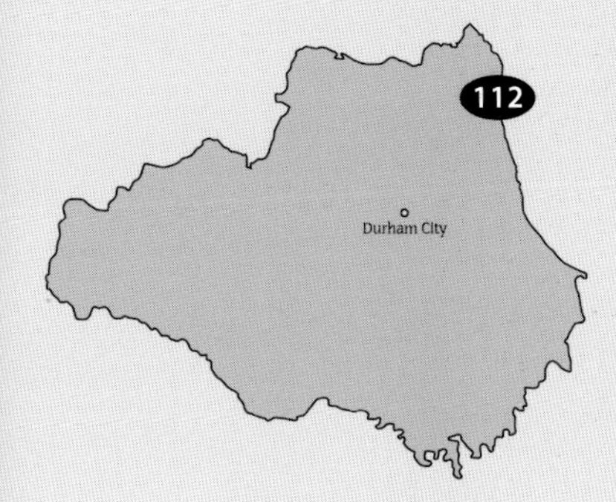

Southwick House

SUNDERLAND. *c.1750 - 1962*

112

Whellan's Directory of 1894 tells us that: *"Southwick is a populous district, formerly at a distance of more than one mile north-west from Sunderland, but is now entirely built up, and is included in the Parliamentary Borough."* The manor passed from the Southwicks to the Hedworths and in 1630 to the Greys of Lumley Castle.

In 1894 Southwick House belonged to Anthony Scott. Scott and his son were earthenware manufacturers and owners of Southwick Pottery. The expansion of Sunderland and the encroachment of industry and housing, including the famous single-storey cottage rows, led to most of the fine Georgian Houses surrounding the green, including Southwick House, being demolished.

Springfield House

SHOTLEY BRIDGE. *c.1840 - 1965*

113

Country houses have often been used for non-domestic purposes at some stage of their lives. Perhaps most commonly they become hotels or restaurants, but in the case of Springfield House the reverse took place. The Springfield Hotel was built in the 1840s to provide accommodation for visitors to Shotley Spa to take the waters. As the stream of visitors to the Spa began to fall it was changed into a private house. After many years as a house it became an orphanage and finally the district headquarters of the National Coal Board. Springfield was demolished in 1965 and replaced by two bungalows. These were also demolished and replaced by luxury apartments called 'The Gables' in 2009.

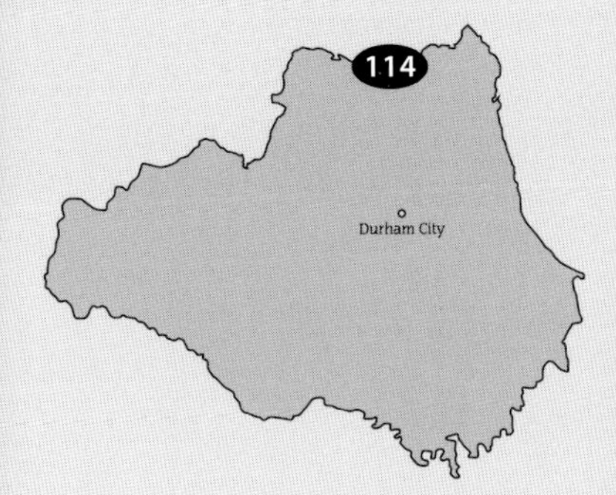

Stella Hall

BLAYDON. *c.1600 - altered C18th - 1840 - 1955*

114

A Nunnery was established here in 1143 and this passed in the Dissolution to the Tempest family in the late sixteenth century. The Tempests, Newcastle merchants, built Stella in 1600 and it was altered in the eighteenth century by James Paine. He altered the fenestration of the front facade, including the Venetian windows which gave so much character to the front. He added pediments to the other windows. John Dobson also worked at the house in 1840.

The house passed in 1850 to Joseph Cowen, chairman of the River Tyne Improvement Commissioners for over twenty years. His son Joseph, radical thinker and newspaper man, entertained many european reformers at Stella. The stone head of the statue of Garibaldi, from Stella, spent many years as a garden feature in a suburban Blaydon garden.

The house was gifted to Durham University by Miss Jane Cowen, last of the family to live in the house, in 1946. They demolished it in 1953. It was replaced by the houses of Stella Park estate. The house is survived by a lodge, gardener's house, estate walling and the grand summer house standing on top of Summer Hill.

115

Durham City

Stella House

BLAYDON. *Early C17th - 1960s*

115

Stella House was home to the Silvertop family for several generations. The family was heavily involved in the coal trade and in 1721 bought the Minsteracres Estate in Northumberland. After extending the original farm house at Minsteracres in two building stages, the second including the installation of water closets (the latest in luxury living) the family left Stella House for Minsteracres. Stella House was gradually reduced in size and the remaining wing turned into a smaller house which, with its remaining Dutch gables, shows what a fine house it was.

Streatlam Castle

BARNARD CASTLE. *Rebuilt 1720 - altered 1841 - gutted 1927 - 1959*

116

John Sykes tells us in his local records: *"In 1424 Streatlam Castle, in the county of Durham, was rebuilt by Sir William Bowes, who was knighted for his valour at the battle of Vernoyle."* This French style castle was kept as the core of an altogether different Streatlam Castle of thirteen bays, the first and last two bays projecting. The roof was given Elizabethan style cupolas over these bays and over the middle two bays. These were originally built of wood but in 1841 replaced by stone.

The castle was largely demolished in 1927 and in 1959 the Territorial Army destroyed the remaining ruin in an army exercise. The Queen Mother picnicked here as a child visiting her Bowes-Lyon relatives, as well as at Gibside the family's other Durham house.

Thrislington Hall

WEST CORNFORTH. *c.1680 - 1979*

117

Whellan's Directory of 1894 lists the owner of Thrislington Hall as William Morson Esq., coal owner and describes the hall as: *"A substantial stone residence occupying a pleasant situation."*

The house was Elizabethan in style, double pile and of three by four bays. The first and third windows on the main three bay front were directly topped by windows of a third half-storey, probably servicing staff bedrooms. The house gradually fell into decline and, after a period of lying empty, was demolished in 1979.

The Tudor House

TANFIELD. *C17th - 1958*

118

Two sides of 'The Square' in old Tanfield village were formed by stone built cottages, echoing similar squares at Newton-by-the-Sea and Mickley in Northumberland. In Tanfield the third side was occupied by the solidly built Tudor House, stone built with typical Elizabethan features. High gables and tall chimney stacks were set off by red pantiled roofs with stone tiled courses at roof level. These were common north-east of England architectural features. The main rooms of the house all contained massive Tudor gothic stone fireplaces and the house boasted both attics and cellars.

It was modernised in the eighteenth century and again in the mid nineteenth. In more recent times the house was used to house a reformatory and plans were put in place to convert it into a village centre for educational and recreational uses. These plans failed to reach fruition and vandalism and theft of architectural features led to demolition in 1958. The houses of Tudor Drive now occupy the site.

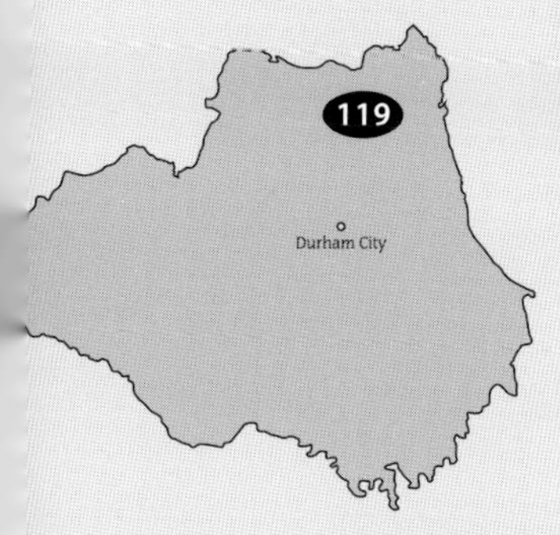

Usworth House (later Peareth Hall)

WASHINGTON. *c.1750 - c.1910*

119

Whellan's Directory tells us that Usworth House *"is a large stone building, situated on an eminence, and commands an extensive view of the surrounding country, including Lambton and Hilton, Sunderland and the sea."*

In 1750 the estate was bought by Newcastle merchant William Peareth and inherited by his son George. This family tenure led to the house becoming known locally as Peareth Hall. In 1894 the house was owned by J. Bailey, Newcastle wine merchant and later to the mine owners of Usworth Colliery.

Finally the house was used as offices for the National Coal Board. The house was demolished circa 1910 with one wing being retained for conversion into Usworth House Farm.

Washington Rectory

WASHINGTON. *c.1720 - 1949*

120

The Rectory was commenced by Richard Stonehewer, rector from 1719 until 1727, to replace the old medieval rectory. The build was completed by George Talbot, rector from 1728 until 1729, later Bishop of Durham, and it was his arms that were placed over the door. The rectory was badly damaged by fire in 1923 but repaired to become the local Urban District Council offices. After a second fire in 1949 the building was demolished and replaced by new council offices. The present rectory was built in 1926.

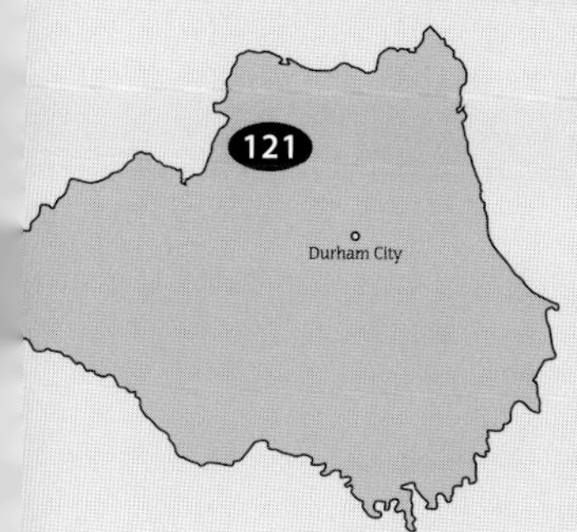

Weed Park

DIPTON. *c.1700s*

121

Weed Park was at the centre of a new estate built up by the Marquis of Bute by buying land from the Swinburne family and Lady Windsor. In the 1840s the house was occupied by Mr. Grey, Lord Bute's agent. This estate was rich in collieries and wagon ways which added to Lord Bute's coal mining interests and also added to his great wealth. This was made even greater by the arrival in the 1850s of the Pontop and Jarrow railway which led to huge growth in the local coal trade.

By the 1890s Weed Park was home to the surgeon Samuel Compton and his daughter Catherine who ran a school for ladies from the house. It ended its life as a home of rest for the elderly.

Weed Park was a rubble built vernacular house of seven bays and a pantiled roof.

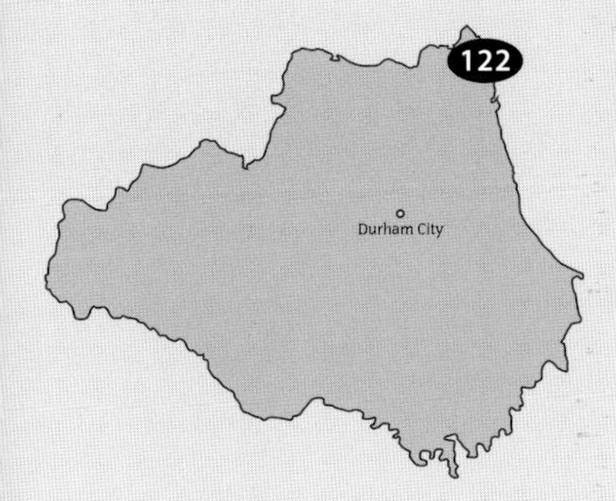

West Hall (formerly West House)

MARSDEN. *Replaced c.1690 - 1953*

122

Whellan's Directory of 1894 Tells us that: " *West Hall, the seat and property of Robert Thompson Esq., J.P., is pleasantly situated on the Cleadon road within wooded grounds. It is a substantial house in the Elizabethan style and is about two hundred years old.*"

Previous owners included Jacob Wilson in 1740 and was sold by the Wilsons to Charles Simpson in 1841. A succession of ship owners followed. West Hall was taken over by the War Department and was used as a hospital during the First World War. During the Second World War it was used to billet soldiers. The house is survived by a lodge on Cleadon Lane.

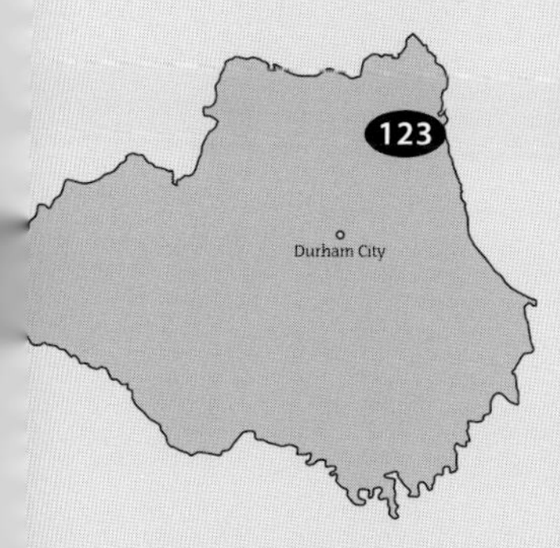

West Herrington Manor House

WEST HERRINGTON.

123

The ancient Manor of Herrington gave name to a local family but in the time of Bishop Bek, Bishop of Durham from 1283 until 1311, the Manor was split into East and West Herrington and these districts remain today, with the more recent addition of Middle Herrington. The Manor was held by many families including the D'Arcys and Hedworths and, in 1680, the Smith family. The early house was demolished circa 1800 and a new house built on a neighbouring site. This building was similar in design to Houghton Hall, three storeys with a flat roof and a castellated parapet.

A pitched roof was added at a later date and the house was subsequently divided into two. In 1938 a group of Sunderland antiquarians visited the house and found a decaying, tenemented building scheduled for demolition.

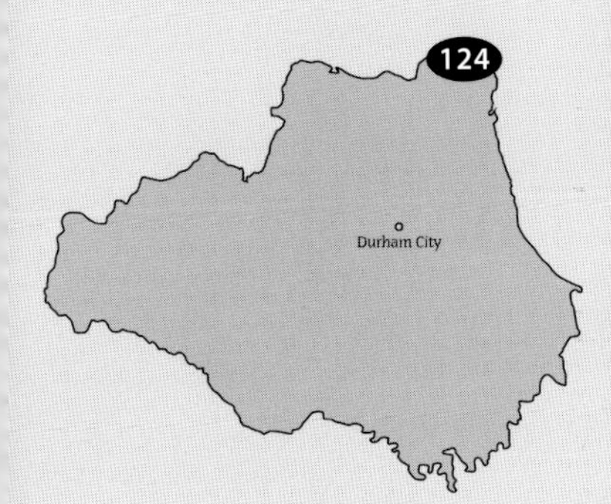

Westoe House

WESTOE. *c.1730 - 1958*

124

Westoe House was an eighteenth century house with a five bay brick front of two storeys, topped by a high plain parapet. Parts of the house dated from the seventeenth century. Westoe was best known as the home of Robert Ingham Q.C., M.P., who had inherited his grandfather's estate in 1824. Ingham was Recorder of Berwick, Member of Parliament for South Shields, Attorney General of the County Palatine of Durham, and was so well respected that he was given a public funeral in 1875. The list of mourners at this event included most of the first families of Tyneside and Durham. The Blacketts, Surtees, Claytons, Blackett-Ordes, Fenwicks, Andersons, Carrs, Carr-Ellisons, together with many representatives of public bodies swelled the large numbers attending the funeral.

The Whaggs

WHICKHAM. *c.1740 - rebuilt 1813 - 1966*

125

William Bourn's Annals of Whickham tells us that on the ninth of October 1750: *"The Rev., Dr. Williamson, of Whickham, was married to Mrs. Barras, of the Whaggs, who is described as an agreeable lady with a fortune above ten thousand pounds."* After marriage the new Mrs. Williamson joined her husband in Whickham Rectory and the Whaggs was offered for rental.

The house consisted of *"nine fine rooms and good and well ceilinged garrets above them, and large arched cellars below, a back kitchen, brew house etc."*

The Whaggs remained in the Williamson family's hands until 1802 when it was purchased by Anthony Leaton and in 1813 was largely rebuilt. It passed through other hands until 1853 when it was bought by Peter Haggie of the Gateshead rope making business.

126

Durham City

Whickham Grange (also known as Burnt House)

WHICKHAM. *1823 -*

126

Whellan's Directory of 1894 tells us: *"Besides the usual village tenements, which are well built and substantial, there are many genteel residences, and in the neighbourhood are several fine mansions, situated in the midst of well-wooded grounds."*

Whickham Grange was one of these mansions. The Grange was built in 1823 by William Taylor whose family first appeared in the Whickham Parish Registers in the sixteenth century. They moved from the Hermitage, built by Matthew Taylor in 1790, which still stands in its beautiful grounds on Whickham Front Street. The Grange and its grounds were covered by the houses of Grange estate.

Whickham House (later Whickham Chase)

WHICKHAM. *c.1710 - 1960*

127

Whickham House was home to the Leaton family for one hundred years. Mr. G. T. Leaton died in 1765 and was succeeded by Anthony Leaton who died in 1803. His son, George Thomas Leaton, inherited and later assumed the surname Leaton-Blenkinsop to gain a further inheritance. George Thomas had made an advantageous marriage as Bourn's Annals of Whickham tells us: *"Married at Eglingham George Thomas Leaton, Whickham House, County Durham Esq., and Miss Harriet Collingwood, Lilburn Tower."*

In 1937 the house was sold to Whickham Urban District Council and used for civil defence purposes during the Second World War. The house was demolished in 1960 but the stable block and ornamental gardens remain and form the beautifully kept Chase Park.

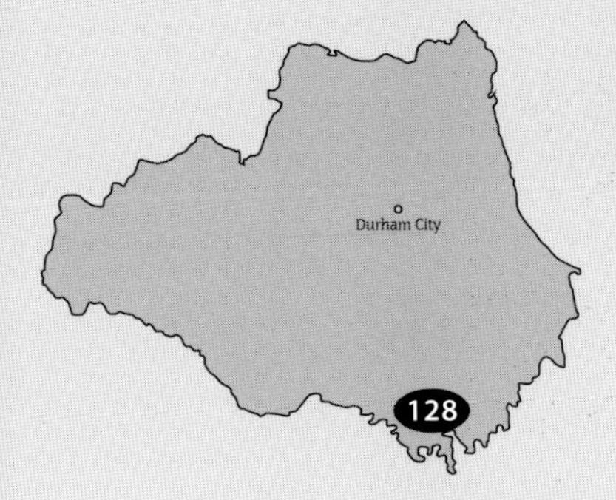

Whinfield

HAUGHTON LE SKERNE.

128

Whellan's Directory of 1894 tells us that: "*Whinfield, the residence and property of John Feetham Esq., J.P., is a fine building of mixed architectural styles. It is situated about two miles east of Darlington and designed by the London architect C. E. Sayer.*"

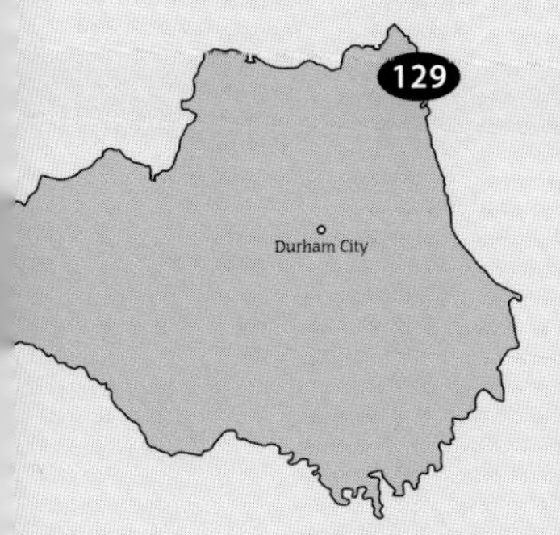

Whitburn Hall

WHITBURN. *c.1600 - 1980*

129

Whitburn Hall was home to the Williamson family from 1719 until 1942, more than two hundred years. Most country houses that have been altered as much as Whitburn are difficult to read architecturally, but at Whitburn the additions are laid out for us in a row. Moving right to left, the original house of 1600 is hidden by trees. An eighteenth century six-bay extension comes next, followed by a nine-bay addition of circa 1800. This range was further altered by John Dobson in 1856 and again in 1880.

This is clearly seen in the second postcard view with its unusual 'Oeil de Boeuf' windows, balustrading and urns in the Baroque style. From 1747 until 1942 every Baronet was known as Sir Hedworth Williamson from the fifth to the ninth Baronets.

Whitehill Hall

CHESTER-LE-STREET. *House mentioned 1310 - rebuilt 1830 - 1917*

130

The Manor of Whitehill was granted in 1310 to Roger De Aula De Cestria by Bishop Beck to hold from the See of Durham for a yearly rental of forty-eight shillings. It next became home to the Millot family from the fourteen hundreds until 1748. Sykes' Local Records tells us that in November 1748: *"This year died John Millot Esq., of Whitehill near Chester-Le-Street. He was a man of very singular habits and conversation."*

The Cooksons owned the estate next and circa 1830 John Cookson rebuilt the house. In 1894 the house was home to Colonel Fife Cookson. By 1917 the estate had been acquired by the Pelton Colliery Company and in that same year Whitehill was demolished. Subsidence was blamed, probably caused by the workings of the neighbouring Pelton Fell collieries.

A new Whitehill was built in 1920 on a neighbouring site but the house was plagued by vandalism. It had a short life, being demolished circa 1965.

White House

HEWORTH. *1344 - 1960*

131

Built on an ancient site White House stood on the foundations of a house mentioned as being in existence in 1344. Perhaps best remembered as the home of Camilla Colville who married Lord Ossulton against his family's wishes. This didn't stop her from becoming Countess of Tankerville on her father-in-law's death. She also became a lady of the bedchamber to Queen Caroline. The Scottish looking house was last inhabited in 1938 and a period of neglect and dereliction was followed by demolition in 1960. The magnificent views of the lower Tyne valley from the site of the house can still be appreciated today. The Whitehills covers the site as does White House Way.

Durham City
132

Whitworth Hall

SPENNYMOOR. *Rebuilt 1845 - rebuilt 1891 - 1900 - became hotel 1998*

132

Whitworth Hall was home to the Shafto family from 1652 until 1981. The old manor house was rebuilt in 1845 with three storeys, seven by five bays, and a three bay conservatory-style library added to the main front. This grand house was destroyed by fire in 1877, only the library wing and kitchen were saved. The house was rebuilt to a smaller plan between 1891 and 1900 by the indomitable Rosa Edith Marguerite Duncombe Shafto, the great, great granddaughter of 'Bonny' Bobby Shafto. She was the last of the Shaftos of Whitworth, leaving in 1981. The new, smaller, more convenient Whitworth Hall became the Best Western Whitworth Hall Hotel in 1998.

Durham City

133

Windlestone - chapel and family

RUSHYFORD.

133

Windlestone Hall, seat of the Eden family, still stands. The early house was rebuilt around 1830 by Sir Robert Johnson Eden, Bart. The expense of the rebuild plus estate building and work on the gardens and parkland cost about forty thousand pounds. Although the Hall remains, the private family chapel no longer exists. The Eden children are shown enjoying a visit to the seaside.

134

Durham City

Wishaw House (formerly Shipcote Villa)

GATESHEAD. *c.1890 - 1990*

134

The above view is of Christ Church, Gateshead, with its original altar table. The five magnificent Chancel windows were given by Major Thomas Dance of Shipcote Villa, Durham Road, Gateshead, later called Wishaw House. The windows were in memory of his wife. The church building had only reached the height of the side windows when funds ran out. Major Dance and Archdeacon Prest, Rector of Gateshead, paid for the completion of Christ Church. Wishaw House was demolished in 1990 and a garage built on its garden. This was later replaced by housing.

Wolviston Hall

WOLVISTON. - *1965*

135

Wolviston Hall occupied the site now covered by the houses of Manor Court and Manor Close. The Hall was also locally known as Webster's Hall after Captain Ernest Webster who bought the estate during the 1880s.

The Websters moved to Unthank Hall, near Haltwhistle in Northumberland, in 1942 and in 1943 Wolviston was made into a prisoner of war camp by the government. After the war the house became apartments and was subsequently replaced by housing in 1965.

The postcard view of the entrance hall at Wolviston shows the typical collection of pictures and prints. Also, the obligatory barometer, exotic plants from the house's huge, famous glass houses and the early central heating system.

Woodburn

DARLINGTON. *1866 -1935*

136

Woodburn was designed by George G. Hoskins for John Pease of East Mount. He also built the neighbouring, and still surviving, Elm Ridge for his daughter Mary Anna Hodgkin, altered into a church in 1932. Woodburn was built for a second daughter, Sophia and her husband Theodore Fry. Fry was a Quaker magnate, Member of Parliament for Darlington between 1880 and 1895, and owner of the Rise Carr Iron Works.

The site of Woodburn is now occupied by the houses of Woodburn Drive built in the late nineteen thirties. Each house nostalgically includes a piece of decorative stone work from the demolished mansion.

Durham City

137

Woodside

DARLINGTON. *1842 - extended c.1850 - 1930*

137

From the 1880s until demolition in 1930 Woodside was home to a branch of the Pease family. This large Quaker family owned many of the Darlington mansions demolished in the 1930s for building land. The vinery and kitchen garden survived and operated as a market garden until 1984 when they too were sacrificed for building purposes. The Woodside estate covered Woodside's grounds. Woodside Drive was the last road to be built. The early Quakers, like the Pease family, were essentially middle class but, by the mid nineteenth century, in the opinion of a Darlington worthy reminiscing in 1861: *"The rich Quakers in my early days were simple in their dress and manners, and lived in moderately sized houses, but these days they have splendid mansions, and carriages, coachmen and footmen etc."*

Woodside Hall

YARM. *1875 - 1935*

138

In Whellan's Directory of 1894 Woodside Hall is listed as one of the seats and residences of the nobility and gentry in the county of Durham. The owner of the house is Richard Henry Appleton Esq., J. P., and mill owner. By the turn of the century Woodside was the home to Sir John Harrison, press man and printer. Woodside was demolished in 1935 and the site used for the building of Cleveland School for Girls. This was later replaced by Teesside High School. The house appears to be a Victorian villa with tower and turret later additions. Close to the house sat a large service court with a grand arched entrance tower.

Wrekenton House

WREKENTON. *c.1815 - 1950s*

139

Wrekenton House was situated on Springwell Road, close to the centre of Wrekenton village. The plain Georgian style house sat in a large walled garden and had a large range of outbuildings, including stables. For most of its life the house was owned by the Davis family, from the mid eighteen hundreds until 1947. In that year Mary Davis, the last of the family died. The Davis family had provided a succession of doctors and surgeons to the area. The house survived until the mid 1950s when it was compulsory purchased by Gateshead Council for a road widening scheme.

County Durham's Lost Houses

The houses indicated in **bold type** are number referenced to the Gazetteer (see pages 12 to 151)

Acorn Close - Sacriston. 1

Ashbrooke Grange - Sunderland

Ashbrooke House (later Corby Hall) - Sunderland. 2

Bainbridge Holme - Sunderland

Beacon Lough - Gateshead

Beaconsfield - Low Fell

Beaurepaire - Bearpark

Beech Holme - Sunderland

Beechwood - Darlington

Belford Villas (later Belford House and Ashcroft) - Sunderland. 3

Benfieldside House - Shotley Bridge. 4

Bensham Cottage - Gateshead

Bensham Hall - Gateshead

Bensham Lodge - Gateshead

Bensham Low House - Gateshead

Bensham Tower - Gateshead

Bent House - South Shields

Biddick Hall Lodge - Washington. 5

Biddick House - South Shields

Billingham Hall - Billingham. 6

Binchester Hall - Binchester ,

Bird Hill House - Whickham. 7

Birtley Hall - Birtley. 8

Birtley House - Birtley

Birtley Old Hall - Birtley

Bishopwearmouth Grange - Sunderland. 9

Bishopwearmouth Rectory - Sunderland. 10

Blackwell Hall - Darlington. 11

Blackwell Hill - Darlington. 12

Blakiston Hall - Wynyard

Blaydon Castle (later Turret Place) - Blaydon. 13

Bloomfield (formerly Walker Villa) - Gateshead

Bradley Hall - Wolsingham. 14

Branksome Hall (formerly Westfield) - Cockerton. 15

Briermede - Gateshead

Brinkburn - Darlington

Broadwood Hall - Satley. 16

Brussleton Tower - St. Helen Auckland. 17

Building Hill House - Sunderland. 18

Bute Hall - Dunston. 19

Carley Lodge - Sunderland

Carr Hill House - Gateshead

Castlegate Corner - Stockton. 20

Chowdene Hall - Gateshead

Claremount House - Gateshead

Cleadon Cottage (later Cleadon Park) - Cleadon. 21

Cleadon Meadows - Cleadon. 22

Cleadon Old Hall - Cleadon. 23

Cocken Hall - Great Lumley. 24

Cockerton Hall - Cockerton

Opposite page: The Gallery, Ravensworth Castle.

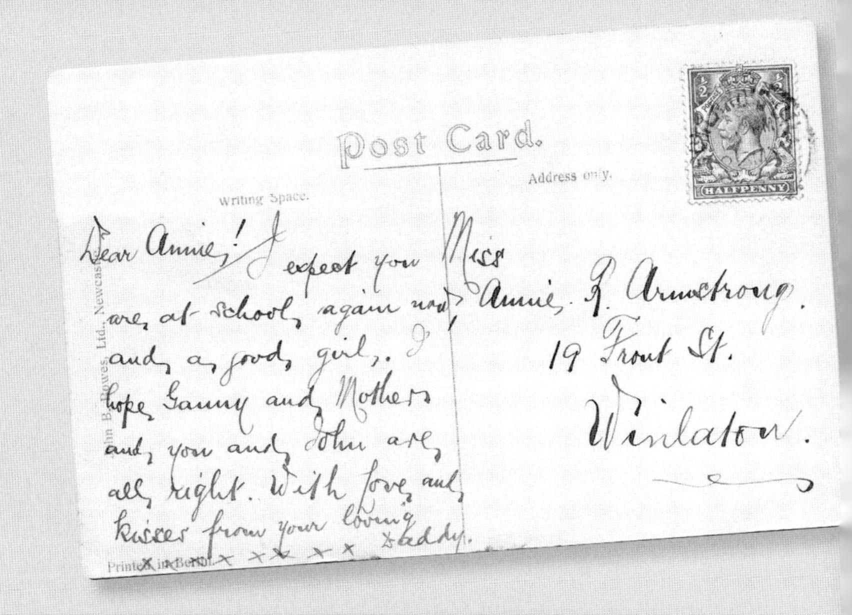
Post Card.

Writing Space.

Address only.

Dear Annie! I expect you are at school again now, and a good girl. I hope Granny and Mothers and you and John are all right. With love and kisses from your loving Daddy.

x x x x x x

Miss Annie R. Armstrong.
19 Front St.
Winlaton.

County Durham's Lost Houses

The houses indicated in **bold type** are number referenced to the Gazetteer (see pages 12 to 151)

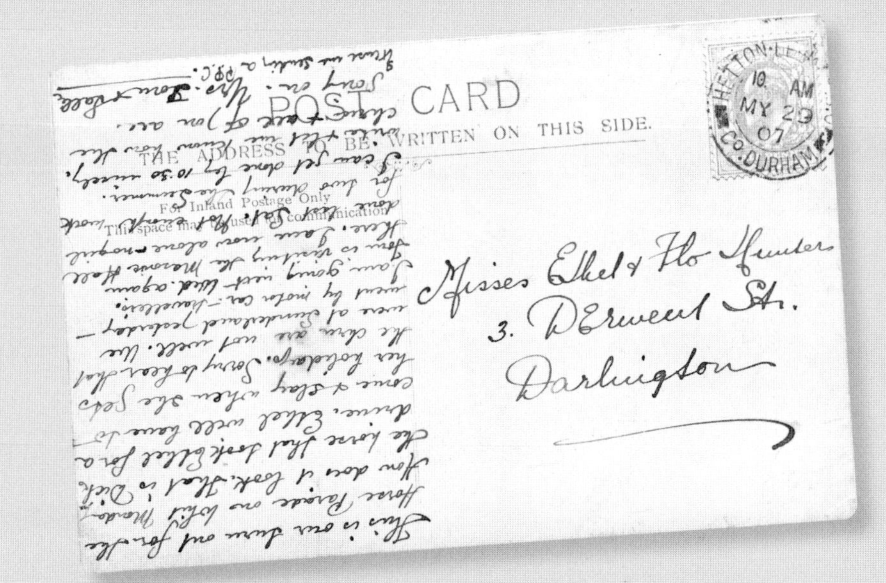

County Durham's Lost Houses

The houses indicated in **bold type** are number referenced to the Gazetteer (see pages 12 to 151)

Greencroft Tower Lodge - Lanchester. 51

Greenesfield House - Gateshead. 52

Greenhill House - Sunderland

Grindon Lodge - Sunderland

Grindon Old Hall - Sunderland. 53

Hardwick Hall: Banqueting House - Sedgefield. 54

Harraton Hall - Washington

Hartburn Hall - Hartburn. 55

Hartlepool Rectory - Hartlepool

Haughton Hall - Haughton-le-Skerne. 56

Hawthorn Tower (formerly Hawthorn Hive Cottage) - Hawthorn. 57

Heathfield: Summer House - Gateshead. 58

Hebburn House - Hebburn

Hedworth Hall - Jarrow

Helmington Hall - Hunwick. 59

Hendon Hill - Sunderland

Hendon House - Sunderland

Hendon Lodge - Sunderland

The Hermitage - Gateshead. 60

Herrington Hall - Middle Herrington. 61

Hetton Hall - Hetton-Ie-Hole. 62

Heworth Rectory - Heworth. 63

High Barnes - Sunderland. 64

Highcroft - Whitburn

Hill Field House - Gateshead

Hollinside - Whickham. 65

Holly House - Gateshead. 66

Holme Lands - Sunderland

Holmeside House - Sunderland

Hoppyland Hall - Bedburn. 67

Houghall Manor House - Durham

Houghton Grange - Houghton-le-Spring

Houghton Grange Summer House - Houghton-le-Spring. 68

Hunters Hall - Sunderland

Hylton Castle - Sunderland. 69

Hylton Grange / Place - Sunderland

Kibblesworth Hall - Kibblesworth

Kibblesworth Old Hall (formerly High Hall, formerly Nether Hall, later The Barracks) - Kibblesworth. 70

Lamb Flatt House. 71 (later Paradise, later Larchfield) - Darlington

Lambton Castle - Washington. 72

Lambton Hall - Washington

Landieu (later Norton House) - Hartburn. 73

Langley Grove - Langley Moor

Langley Hall - Langley Park. 74

Langton Grange - Ingleton. 75

Lawe House (formerly Cross House) - South Shields

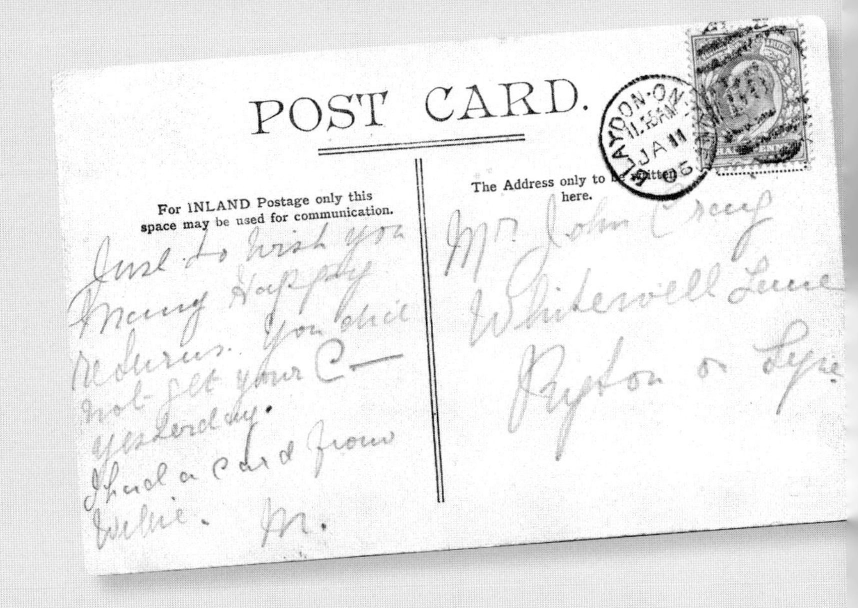

County Durham's Lost Houses

The houses indicated in **bold type** are number referenced to the Gazetteer (see pages 12 to 151)

Laygate House - South Shields

Leafield - Birtley. 76

Leechmere House (later Leechmere Hall) - Sunderland. 77

The Limes - Sunderland

Little Usworth Hall - Washington. 78

Long Newton Hall - Long Newton

Low Barnes (later Pembertons) - Sunderland. 79

Low Butterby Manor House - Croxdale

Ludworth Tower - Ludworth

Mainsforth Hall - Bishop Middleham. 80

Marley Hill House - Marley Hill

Marsden Cottage (later Salmon's Hall) - Marsden

Medomsley Hall - Medomsley. 81

Mill House - Jarrow

Monkwearmouth Grange - Sunderland

Monkwearmouth Hall - Sunderland

Moorhill - Sunderland

Moor House - West Rainton. 82

The Mount - Darlington. 83

The Mount - Ryton

Muggleswick Grange - Muggleswick

Neasham Hall - Neasham. 84

Nest House - Felling

Nettlesworth Hall - Nettlesworth

Newton Cap Hall(s) - Bishop Auckland. 85

Newton Hall - Durham. 86

North Biddick Hall (later Cook's Hall) - Washington. 87

North Hall - Sunderland

North Leam - Heworth

Norton Hardwick - Stockton—on-Tees

Norton House - Norton. 88

Number 8, Hall Terrace - Gateshead. 89

Oakfield - Gateshead

Offerton Manor House - Offerton

Old Axwell - Winlaton Mill

Old Durham - Durham

Old Park Hall - Byers Green. 90

Oswald House - Durham

Owton Manor - West Hartlepool

Pallion Hall - Sunderland. 91

Parkhead Hall (formerly Derwent Villa) - Winlaton. 92

Park House - Sunderland

Park View - Gateshead

Peareth Grove (later Claremont House) - Sunderland

Pelton Vicarage - Pelton. 93

Prospect House - Chester-le-Street. 94

Ragworth Hall - Norton

Rainton Hall - West Rainton

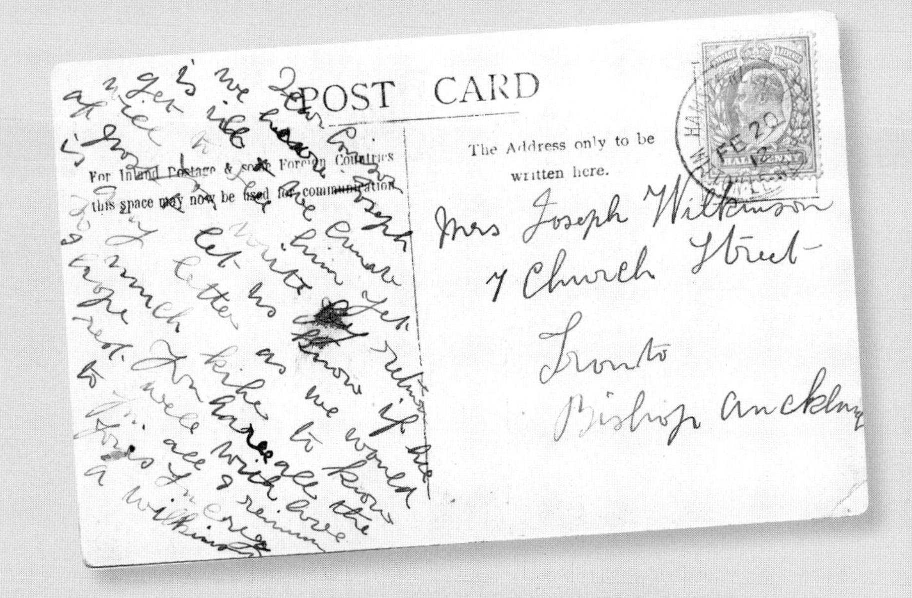

County Durham's Lost Houses

The houses indicated in **bold type** are number referenced to the Gazetteer (see pages 12 to 151)

Rainton House - East Rainton

Ravenshill - Gateshead

Ravensworth Castle - Lamesley. 95

Ravensworth Castle: Alms Houses - Lamesley. 96

Ravensworth Cottage - Dunston. 97

Ravensworth Villa - Gateshead

Redby House - Sunderland

Red Hall - Haughton-le-Skerne. 98

Redheugh Hall - Gateshead. 99

Red House - High Etherley. 100

Rockcliffe - Westoe

Rock Lodge - Sunderland

Rodsley House - Gateshead

Roecliffe (later Redhill) - Whitburn

Rogerley Hall - Frosterley

Romulus House - Gateshead

Runhead House - Ryton

Ryhope Hall - Sunderland. 101

Ryton House - Ryton. 102

Sacriston Heugh - Sacriston

St. Helen Auckland Manor House
- St. Helen Auckland

Saltwell Hall - Gateshead. 103

Saltwell Vale - Low Fell

Seaton Carew Vicarage - Seaton Carew. 104

Sherburn Hall - Sherburn. 105

Sherburn Tower - Rowlands Gill. 106

Sheriff Hill Hall - Gateshead. 107

Shield Row Hall - Stanley

Shipcote House - Gateshead. 108

Silksworth Old Hall - Sunderland

Simonside Hall - South Shields

Snotterton Hall - Staindrop.109

South Close - Gateshead

South Dene Tower - Gateshead. 110

South Hetton Hall - South Hetton. 111

South Hill - Gateshead

Southwick House - Sunderland. 112

Springfield - Gateshead

Springfield House - Shotley Bridge. 113

Stanley Hall - Stanley

Stella Hall - Blaydon. 114

Stella House - Blaydon. 115

Streatlam Castle - Barnard Castle. 116

Summerfield - Gateshead

Team Lodge (later Endsleigh) - Gateshead

Team Villa - Dunston

Tees Grange - Darlington

Thompson's Hall - South Shields

Thornfield - Sunderland

Thornhill House (formerly Plenty Hall) - Sunderland

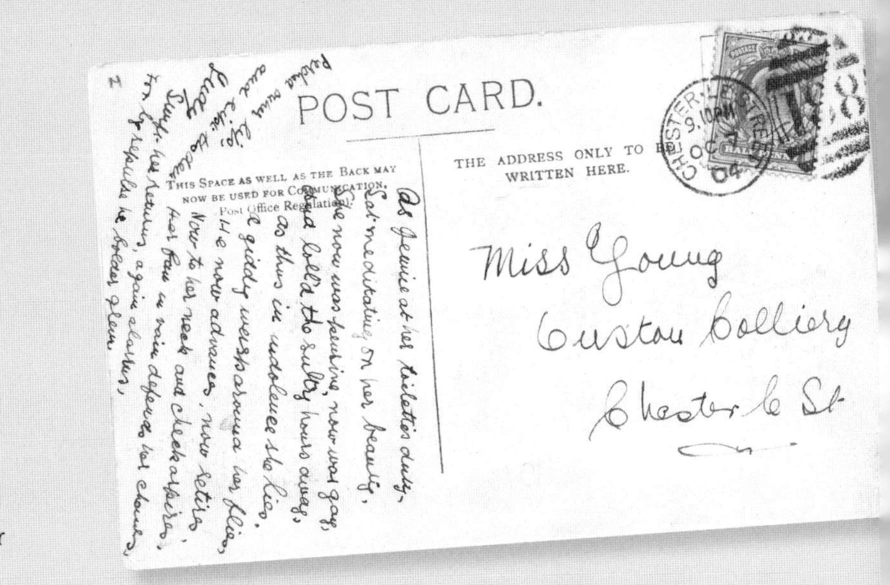

County Durham's Lost Houses

The houses indicated in **bold type** are number referenced to the Gazetteer (see pages 12 to 151)

Thornlea - Sunderland

Thrislington Hall - West Cornforth. 117

Trimdon Old Hall - Trimdon

The Tudor House - Tanfield.118

Tunstall Court - West Hartlepool

Tunstall Manor - West Hartlepool

Tynevale House - Gateshead

Uplands - Darlington

Usworth House (later Peareth Hall) - Washington. 119

Wardley Manor House - Wardley

Washington Rectory - Washington. 120

Weed Park - Dipton. 121

West Hall (formerly West House) - Marsden. 122

West Herrington Manor House. - West Herrington 123

West Hetton Lodge - Coxhoe

Westoe House - Westoe. 124

West Rainton Manor House - West Rainton

West View House - Gateshead

The Whaggs - Whickham. 125

Whessoe Grange - Whessoe

Whickham Grange (later Burnt House) - Whickham. 126

Whickham House (later The Chase). - Whickham 127

Whinfield - Haughton-le-Skerne. 128

Whitburn Hall - Whitburn. 129

Whitehill Hall - Chester-le-Street. 130

White House - Blaydon

White House - Heworth. 131

Whitworth Hall - Spennymoor. 132

Windlestone Chapel - Rushyford. 133

Winlaton Hall - Winlaton

Wishaw House (formerly Shipcote Villa). - Gateshead 134

Wolviston Hall - Wolviston. 135

Woodburn - Darlington. 136

Woodcroft Hall - Stanhope

Woodside - Darlington. 137

Woodside Hall - Yarm. 138

Wrekenton House - Wrekenton. 139

Opposite page: The Drawing Room, Lambton Castle.

White House, Heworth.

Designed and produced by Design Station, Cumbria.
Email: design@amillington.plus.com

Printed by Biddles Books Ltd, Kings Lynn.
www.biddles.co.uk

First published in March 2022 by
Wagtail Press,
Gairshield, Steel, Hexham,
Northumberland, NE47 0HS.

www.wagtailpress.uk
Email: wagtailpress@yahoo.co.uk

Also available from Jim Davidson and Wagtail Press:

Northumberland's Lost Houses
ISBN: 978-0-9559395-8-7

Northumberland's Lost Houses
A picture postcard history by Jim Davidson

WAGTAIL PRESS

ISBN: 978-0-9559395-9-4